Unspoken Wisdom

Unspoken Wisdom

Truths My Father Taught Me

RAY S. ANDERSON

Augsburg
MINNEAPOLIS

UNSPOKEN WISDOM
Truths My Father Taught Me

Scripture quotations are from the New Revised Standard Version Bible, copyright
© 1989 by the Division of Christian Education of the National Council of the
Churches of Christ in the USA and used by permission.

Excerpt from "The Hollow Men" in *Collected Poems 1909-1962* by T. S. Eliot, copyright 1936 by Harcourt Brace & Company, copyright © 1964, 1963 by T. S. Eliot,
reprinted by permission of Harcourt Brace & Company and Faber and Faber Ltd.

"Closing In" from *The Unicorn and Other Poems* by Anne Morrow Lindbergh, copy-
right © 1956 by Anne Morrow Lindbergh. Copyright renewed 1984 by Anne
Morrow Lindbergh. Reprinted by permission of Pantheon Books, a division of
Random House, Inc.

"Sonnet X" of *Epitaph for the Race of Man* by Edna St. Vincent Millay. From *Collected
Poems*, HarperCollins. Copyright © 1934, 1962 by Edna St. Vincent Millay and
Norma Millay Ellis. Reprinted by permission of Elizabeth Barnett, literary executor.

"A Sleep of Prisoners" from *Three Plays* by Christopher Fry, copyright © 1961
Oxford University Press. Reprinted by permission.

Cover design and photo: Ann Elliot Artz

Library of Congress Cataloging-in-Publication Data

Anderson, Ray Sherman.
    Unspoken Wisdom : truths my father taught me / Ray S. Anderson.
        p.   cm.
    ISBN 0-8066-2811-1 (pbk. : alk. paper)
    1. Christian life. 2. Life. 3. Fathers and sons. 4. Parent and child. 5. Farm life—
South Dakota. 6. South Daokta—Social life and customs. 7. Anderson, Ray
Sherman. I. Title.
BV4501.2.A4746   1995
248.8'45—dc20   94-44754
                                                                           CIP

The paper used in this publication meets the minimum requirements of American
National Standard for Information Sciences—Permanence of Paper for Printed
Library Materials, ANSI Z329.48-1984.   ∞™

Manufactured in the U.S.A.   AF 9-2811

98   97   96   95   1   2   3   4   5   6   7   8   9   10

Contents

Introduction / 9

one　　Where your hand is, let your heart
be also / 11

two　　Facing your fear and finding your
confidence / 21

three　　Finding a solution rather than fixing
blame / 30

four　　It is easier to do it right the first time / 39

five　　Putting your faith in the seed and not in
the harvest / 50

six　　Living by your convictions, even when they
are costly / 60

seven　　Follow the curve and contour your life to
the land / 71

eight　　Let the rhythm of life carry some of the
risk / 80

nine　　Being who you are is all you need to be / 89

ten　　Moving out from another's shadow into
your own sun / 98

eleven　　Learning to live means learning to die / 108

twelve　　The cows still stand up at midnight on
Christmas Eve / 118

introduction

y father lived and died as a farmer in South Dakota and, to my knowledge, strayed no more than a hundred miles or so from his birthplace. He was strongly attached to the soil from which he came and in which he was finally laid to rest. He did not talk about farming as a calling in life. He simply made no distinction between what he did for a living and his identity as a person.

Being Norwegian (and Lutheran), he could have fit comfortably in the cast of characters created by Garrison Keillor in the popular program *A Prairie Home Companion.*

My father's language of love was largely nonverbal. When he spoke, the words were seldom aimed directly at me, though they were meant for me to hear. Most often there were no words, only a space by his side where I fit nicely. He was a quiet man, but not a narrow person.

When he was in the field, his soul was as wide as the sweeping South Dakota horizon. In the barn, with his head nestled against the side of the cow he was milking, or currying the sweat-matted hair of the horses as they relished their ration of oats, he was as circumscribed and composed as the creatures he tended.

In the home, my father demanded no special position, only a worn, leather-lined rocker where he relaxed after evening chores. His favorite reading was the *Saturday Evening Post.* He chuckled out loud at the most recent antics of the caterpillar salesman whose exploits were recounted in a series of "letters with the home office." That, as far as I know, was the extent of his literary diet. He had first chance at the *Post* (we all knew that), and first claim on the rocker (his only reward for a full day's work). That simple ritual of reading stimulated my own appetite for the printed word. For if words could make my father laugh out loud, they had a power that tantalized me!

When I was found sitting in his chair, he simply moved me by taking me by one ear and leading me to another! I do not recall this as a punishment or a painful thing; rather as a time when I felt his touch. And, at this distance, it seems more like a bond between us than if he had caressed my cheek.

Personal anecdotes about my father will serve as the story line of this book. But this is not a book about fathers, nor only about father-son relationships, though I use both in developing the theme of each chapter. It is really about how the relationship of parents with children shapes personal character and values.

What I have to share is deeply rooted in my own experience, but it is as universal and relevant as every person's struggle to achieve competence in accepting life as both a gift and a task.

My hope is that from my stories both fathers and mothers will learn how to be more effective in the lives of their children. I also hope that men and women will find in this book a reflection of their own experiences. Each of us has an anecdotal history as well as a chronological one.

My desire is that the telling of my stories will awaken stories that each of us has to remember and share. And, above all, that our lives will provide experiences that will become stories in the lives of others—stories that teach what it is to know life as gift and task.

Where your hand is, let your heart be also

wo sandwiches, a cookie or piece of cake, and a small thermos of coffee, twice a day—mid-morning and mid-afternoon. This was my father's lunch when he was working in the field. At the age of six or seven, it was usually my task—and not an unhappy one—to carry this repast out to him.

These were the days when farm implements were drawn by horses. While my father quietly ate his lunch, I would pet the horses. On occasion, I would slip a sugar cube stolen from my mother's cupboard into the mouth of my favorite horse, enjoying the slobbering lips against my palm as much as the animal relished the sweet cube.

By the time my father had finished the sandwiches and poured his second cup of coffee, I was back at his side, strategically placed for a ritual I had come to expect. Eyeing the piece of cake thoughtfully, he would say, "Well, son, I'm not sure I'm up to the cake today. Could you eat it for me while I roll a cigarette?"

While he performed his little ritual—shaking a measured amount of tobacco out of a small cloth sack onto the thin paper, licking the edges with his lips and striking a match on the sole of his shoe to light the cigarette—I devoured the cake.

The cigarette seemed to lighten the load for him as well as

loosen his tongue. When he talked it was usually as much to him-self as it was to me. My role was to listen. It was not, you might say, a real conversation: neither man to man, nor man to boy. At the same time, in its own way, those times were intensely rela-tional, as I now look back upon them.

He talked about the horses. Each had a name so that they could be startled out of their laggard ways by a shout and maybe a touch of the whip when pulling the plow. Like Santa's rein-deer, horses responded to their names and their master's voice.

"Star [named for the white splash on his otherwise brown face] is limping a bit. I think we better take a look at his hoof tonight. Might have a stone in it." That was a promise, of course. And that evening we—he and I—would examine the foot and perform the simple operation of removing the stone.

The "we" was my father's language of love. He often used it when speaking of his life and tasks, including me as a partici-pant. "We will plant corn in this field next year," he would say, as though I needed to know in order to make my own plans accordingly!

At those times I was not just a boy who carried his lunch, but a partner in his enterprise. He had no need—indeed, no lan-guage—to "talk down" to me. Nor did he attempt to treat me as a man with the pretense of "man talk."

What a marvelous word is "we"! While inclusive, it is able to allow for the difference between "you" and "me," equalizing any disparity of age, gender, race, and even religion. What I did when I was alone or with other kids never seemed of much inter-est to my father. If entering into the games of their children and becoming their cheerleader are skills of parenting, my father was woefully deficient. He excelled, however, in the ageless wis-dom of "we" talk—a skill that drew me into countless exciting partnerships with him.

My young life was narrow and my pursuits were trivial. My

peers were competitors as much as they were companions or partners. My siblings were rivals as much as relatives. Yet, my father's utterance of "we" forged a father-and-son bond as deep and broad as our common destiny on earth, a bond that bound man and boy in one struggle between faith and fate.

With utter unself-consciousness, he drew me out of my own childhood into a common life and destiny without destroying the child in me. Perhaps it was out of this unconscious and unspoken wisdom that he was prompted to do something that forever transformed my life.

A ONCE-IN-A-LIFETIME GIFT

It happened only once. There was no suggestion that it was planned or premeditated. We were sitting on the edge of a furrow behind the plow, facing the freshly turned soil over which sea gulls swooped in search of worms. It was second-cup-of-coffee time. A newly lit cigarette had loosened his tongue.

"Stick your hand down into the soil, son," he suddenly said, breaking the rules by looking into my face and talking directly to me. As I did, he said softly, "Son, this soil is part of your life—you take care of it and it will take care of you."

No response was expected, of course. Nor did I give one—I knew the rules and lived by ritual as well. He said no more and he never spoke of it again. I never questioned him about its meaning. It may have been a premonition on his part, of his own transition from a tiller of the soil into a part of the soil itself. Or it may have simply been the only gift that he knew how to give me: the wisdom of desire being fulfilled in destiny.

It was, you might say, my once-in-a-lifetime gift.

The incident with my father was forgotten during my teenage years. These were days of war and rumors of war. With Pearl Harbor and the plunge into the Second World War, my high-school days were preoccupied with thoughts of impending military service. Immediately following my eighteenth birthday, I enlisted in the Army Air Force and left that fall for the service.

With the end of the war, I returned to the family farm and, for the first time, found stirring in me an attraction to the soil that brought back the memory of my father's words. I never spoke of them to him, of course. We still had no common language for such talk.

Strangely, though my father's words had bound me to the soil his insistence that I leave the farm and go to college precipitated my next departure from the soil. There was a bit of a quarrel over this, I recall. I had hoped to help him run the farm and thus begin to build up my own farming operation.

"There is not room enough for both of us," he said. "Why not go off to college and get an education? That is the one thing that I never had an opportunity to do. You can always farm, but you cannot always have this opportunity."

I left in a huff, not realizing how wise and freeing his words were. At the same time, my sense of attachment to the soil only seemed to grow stronger. While in college, I earned a degree in agricultural science and worked part-time in the college's farm operations. During my last year, I sold the new car I had purchased with money saved during my military service and bought a tractor. Arrangements were made to rent a farm back in the community in which I was raised. I did the fall plowing and then went back to college to finish my final year. In the spring, I took my own new family and moved to the farm.

That spring, as I was milking the cows in the barn of my rented farm, my parents arrived for a visit. My father sat on a stool watching me for a time. Then he quietly said, "Son, it seems that you have finally found what you want in life."

My answer was brief and affirmative. "Yes, Dad, this is where I belong." My father had retired from his own farm several years earlier because of ill health. It was as though our roles were reversed: he was now the boy sitting beside the man. He did not say it, but I think he was silently asking, "Son, are you and I still 'we'?"

Flushed with the excitement of my new venture in life, I did not have the wisdom to sense his searching question. If I had, I might have responded: "This fall, I think we will need to remodel this barn to make room for more cows."

Instead, that fall, he quietly died of the cancer that ate away the tissue of his throat and destroyed his voice box so that he could hardly speak. The same cigarettes that had lightened his load and loosened his tone had the final word in the end.

✗ TRANSPLANTING—ROOTS AND ALL

There is a saying that is as old as the hills: "You can take the boy out of the farm, but you cannot take the farm out of the boy." I took this as conventional wisdom and a kind of "manifest destiny" for my life. I even added a paraphrased version that went something like this: "You can take the boy out of or away from the father, but you cannot take the father out of the boy."

For seven years I pursued my vision and vocation of farming, tracing out my destiny in the good earth. The legacy of my father became the lengthened shadow of my own place in the sun. To my passion for the soil I added a fascination with modern technology and the exhilaration of buying and using the latest in farm equipment. I bought and sold, planted and reaped, suffered failure and enjoyed success.

Why was it not enough? Was this not my destiny, to wrestle the soil into submission even while it was working its magic in my heart?

An idea came into my mind like a plant fully grown, with no need for soil preparation and planting. I awoke one day and knew that something was pulling me toward a future that had no antecedent in my past (or so I thought). With the revitalizing of a personal faith in God that had long lain dormant, I found compelling and unavoidable inspiration in the words of Jesus Christ.

The New Testament Gospel of Luke describes how Jesus told a story of a farmer who kept building bigger barns to store the wealth of his harvests. In concluding the story, Jesus said: "But God said to [the farmer]: 'You fool! This very night your life is being demanded of you. And the things you have prepared, whose will they be?' So it is with those who store up treasures for themselves but are not rich toward God."

For more than a year, I struggled with what seemed to be two competing and irresolvable demands upon my life: my love of farming and my desire to serve God. In theory, I had no problem with the idea that one could serve God through farming as well as through any other vocation. But one is not always able to apply theory to life. I knew enough about the Bible to establish theological permission for my calling to be a farmer and thereby live out a gift given to me by my father.

What I couldn't discover in the Bible was inner certainty that farming would ultimately fulfill my passion for life. Frankly, I was as much troubled about the potential outcome of my life as a farmer as I was tormented by the thought that God had other plans for me. When I finally decided to leave the farm to prepare for a vocation as pastor and (eventually) teacher, it was not because I heard specific instructions from God. Life is seldom as simple as that.

Instead, a growing life of faith that included Christian friends and a community of love and fellowship began to open a door of awareness that could never again be closed. Through this door my passion spilled out like a river that overruns its banks. At the same time, once this door was open, warm breezes blew in and swept over sleeping segments of my soul. I awakened to what I thought was the sound of God talking, as if to himself, yet knowing that I was present: "Tomorrow, we will go to those who are like sheep without a shepherd and bring them to a safe place." It was the "we" in God's words that reached out and included me!

Years later, when I read the words of Christopher Fry, I could see in them my own experience, my own awakening to God's "we."

> The human heart can go to the lengths of God,
> Dark and cold we may be, but this
> Is no winter now. The frozen misery
> Of centuries breaks, cracks, begins to move;
> The thunder is the thunder of the floes,
> The thaw, the flood, the upstart Spring.
> Thank God our time is now when wrong
> Comes up to face us everywhere,
> Never to leave us till we take
> The longest stride of soul men ever took,
> Affairs are now soulsize.
> The enterprise
> Is exploration into God.

> ("A Sleep of Prisoners," *Three Plays*, New York: Oxford University Press, 1961, p. 209)

And so we left, my family and I, for another state and another life, not daring to look back—not for fear that one of us would turn into a pillar of salt, but that our respect for the dead (though still alive in us) would weaken resolve to reach the new frontier.

In making the decision to leave the farm and sever my connection with the soil, I fully expected to suffer, not regret, but melancholy. It would be, I thought, a kind of death that would leave part of me unattached. In a sense, I felt I was leaving behind my father as well as the soil.

I was pleasantly surprised to discover, even after only a few months, that my new "calling" to study for the Christian ministry had not left an empty space. Nor did I long for what had been or what might have been. What I had expected to be a painful uprooting turned out to be a transplant—roots and all—from one soil to another.

What my father had discovered, but left for me to learn on my own, was that there was neither mystery nor magic in the soil. The mystery and magic, if we dare to use such words, lie in the connection of the heart to the hand. There is no place or task on earth satisfying to the restless hand that is not attached to the heart.

On that day long ago, my father had not attached my hand to the soil of a farm—although that was how I had understood it. Rather, he had attempted to attach my hand to my heart. No matter what "soil" my hand was plunged into, if the task was undertaken with my heart, there was a sense of completeness that brought joy and fulfillment. My father's once-in-a-lifetime gift was the ability to grow in any soil, the ability to be not only transplanted but transformed—by loving what I do.

THE TRANSFORMING POWER OF THE "WE" OF GOD

How do we account for the shift of passion from one objective to another? How do we explain the inner certainty with which we change direction without doubting the correctness of the first objective and without questioning the rightness of the next?

Did I unknowingly stumble into some kind of "transforming power" through which I reached for more than the soil could offer? It is surely a paradox that my father both taught me that my integrity could be measured by how straight I planted a row of corn and also empowered me to reach out for fulfillment in the world that ended beyond the last row of corn.

I did not leave my father sitting on a stool, retired from farming and waiting for me to give him a life. Nor did I betray him by pulling my plow out of the ground and leaving the farm without his permission. At one time, part of me thought that way, but no more.

The "we" that I discovered in God has room for both my father and me. When God whispered, "Tomorrow, we will go to those who are like sheep without a shepherd," I became God's partner. The "we" of God equalizes our relationship without confusing or distorting the difference between us. Like my father, God does not talk down to me, as a man to a child; nor does God attempt to treat me as divine with the pretense of "God talk."

In the New Testament Gospel of John, Jesus tells his closest followers: "I do not call you servants . . . but I have called you friends, because I have made known to you everything that I have heard from my Father." And Jesus promises them: "Those who love me will keep my word, and my Father will love them; and we will come to them and make our home with them."

We will come to them and make our home with them! There it is. The transforming power of the "we" of God!

I have to say this: my father on earth prepared me to become a partner of God by also empowering me to live as a partner within his own "we." The transforming power of such inclusive love is in its empowering of the "I" through partnership in the "We."

As long as we stand outside of that partnership, our lives bear more of a burden than any one of us can carry. Even God becomes our competitor. We always lose in such a match, and God can't win either.

As you are beginning to see, this book is not merely about

my father nor is it only about a father-son relationship. The power of the "we" relationship that was my father's gift to me is not gender-specific or role-related. The understanding of vocation and fulfillment as a bond of hand and heart is not limited to the soil of a farm, nor to a father's expectations of his son. It happened that my father worked the soil as God's partner, though he would have been uncomfortable to make that claim for himself. This was the transforming power of his life. And I touched an understanding of that power as I stood with him, a partner—part of his "we"—who joined in his struggles with faith and with fate.

Now, wherever I put my hand, my heart is bound to follow. And I have discovered the secret of fulfillment and happiness. My father on earth and my Father in heaven are now part of my "we," and they clasp their hands in joy.

Facing your fear and finding your confidence

he horse was not "user-friendly," to borrow an expression from the computer culture. I didn't like the look in its eyes. Maybe it was because it had never worked a day in its life. The horses I had come to know on my father's farm were all used to working the soil. They had an honest, you-can-trust-me look about them.

This horse belonged to a family who lived in town and had made arrangements to have it boarded at our farm for their son to ride. It was a high-spirited animal, with slender, prancing legs and a long neck which arched with arrogance. I was not afraid of horses, having worked with them from the time I was old enough to help with the chores around the barn. But I was afraid of this horse and, I believe, with good reason. For each time that the father brought his son Wally out to ride the horse, the animal became uncontrollable. When the boy got on, the horse would rear and paw the ground as though gearing up to run the Kentucky Derby.

I was probably twelve or thirteen years old at the time. We had six horses which were used in the fields during the week. On Sunday, I was permitted to ride the smallest one, and I spent many a pleasant afternoon exploring the countryside with the horse. In the summer, the horse was my frequent companion as I herded cows in the open fields when fenced pastures were dry and sparse. I was not big enough to mount a horse without a boost from someone or a nearby fence from which I could jump on.

One afternoon, Wally came out to the farm with his father to make another attempt at riding. I remember the occasion vividly. Fear has a way of making vivid, lasting impressions.

My father led the horse out of the barn and handed the reins to Wally. The boy was paralyzed and looked to his father for help. A brief discussion ensued about the likelihood of the horse throwing Wally out of the saddle. The result was an impasse. The horse arched his neck and pawed at the ground. Wally stood petrified and silent. His father grew impatient and angry.

At that moment, to my consternation, I heard my father say, "Well, why don't we have Ray take the horse out for a little ride and calm him down. Ray can do it."

"No, Dad. Not this horse. Not this time," I wanted to say. But his quiet confidence in me was irresistible. Without a moment's hesitation, I said, "Sure, give me a boost." And suddenly there I was, perched on top of 1,400 pounds of quivering, nervous muscle, raring to go.

I turned the horse on a dime (actually it was the horse that managed it, his front legs already being in the air!), and we headed down the road at a reasonably controlled speed. I remember feeling rather confident. Perhaps my fear had been misplaced.

Then it happened. The moment I turned the horse to head back to the barn, the animal seized the bit in its teeth and pushed into overdrive. I was helpless. Any attempt to control the horse was hopeless. What little skill I had, plus the sheer instinct for survival, somehow enabled me to stay on the horse.

There was a minor problem, however. As the barn loomed larger in my vision, I realized that the horse had no plans for a controlled approach. We either were going to hit the barn head-on or the horse was going to make a panic stop. The decision was not mine, so I prepared for either.

As it turned out, the animal was not stupid. At the very last second it planted its feet and skidded to an abrupt stop. As I went hurtling over the top of the horse's head I remember thinking, "Land on your feet, Ray." And I did! On an Olympic scale I would rate it a 9.5.

"That's a nice horse," I said somewhat breathlessly as I strolled over to my father. "It just needs to be ridden more." Was I non-chalant or what?

Well, in retrospect, I suppose that I gave myself a bit more credit than I actually deserved. I doubt that I fooled my father, but it did make an impression on Wally and his dad!

I must add that, even though I managed to ride the horse that one time, I had no intention of repeating the experience. Courage always has fear as a riding partner. And wisdom can see through a lucky, successful dismount. I left my fear with that horse and went on with my life. As I recall, Wally's father sold the horse soon after and that was the end of the matter.

⚔ TAKING YOUR FEAR FOR A RIDE

Why do I remember this incident so clearly even now? Not simply because of the fear I felt. I have had many instances where I was terrified. The clue to this incident's lasting impression is the one line uttered by my father: "Ray can do it."

This was not the first time my father had put me in a position where I was expected to do something that seemed beyond my capabilities. However, I never failed to rise to his challenges—no matter how unrealistic they might have appeared to my young mind. And I'm certain that this was because, along with his expectations, my father always managed to convey total confidence in me.

It is the confidence that another has in us that empowers and gives courage. When expectations are placed on us without the implied confidence that we can meet them, we feel disempowered and discouraged. The very word "encouragement" implies that courage can be developed through the projection of confidence.

What I recall most vividly about this incident is the *expressed* confidence that my father showed when he said: "Ray can do it." Because I had experienced so many times his unspoken trust, my self-confidence was strong enough that his statement did not produce terror in me. Rather, it fortified me and gave me the courage to take my fear for a ride.

Those who specialize in developmental psychology tell us how important key experiences are in forming our self-identity. There is often something in such experiences that becomes internalized as a building block in our self-concept.

In the incident with the horse, my fear of the animal could no longer be kept at a safe distance. As long as I was not expected to ride the horse, I could avoid dealing with the fear, secretly happy that it was Wally's horse and not mine. My self-confidence could remain intact, based on familiarity with horses that I knew and trusted.

Once my father said "Ray can do it," however, the demand upon my self-confidence increased by a quantum leap! The test was no longer my ability to avoid that horse, but my faith—my confidence—in my father. To beg off from riding would show that I had no confidence in my father's judgment. That would have been the first time that I had ever distrusted him. And my self-confidence was largely based on his trust in me.

What we call self-confidence is not based on our ability to perform but on the trust we have that our performance will *not* be the sole basis of our acceptance and value to others.

I have friends who feel they were crippled in the development of their self-confidence because they were always expected to perform for the sake of gaining approval. Whether the performance was academic, athletic, artistic, or vocational, the standard was always raised a notch following each success.

One man told me that he quit the track-and-field team in college because every training session ended in a failure. No matter how high he jumped, the bar was always raised a notch until he missed. Failure was the last experience of the day. The coach called it motivation, but the college student saw it as missing the mark.

THE POWER OF ENCOURAGEMENT

Let me return to the issue of trust as it relates to self-confidence. My father gave me the feeling that I could be trusted to take on tasks that required more competence and skill than I already had acquired. It was taking responsibility for doing something, not the performance itself, that became his measure of me. Failure to perform perfectly was part of learning to do something well, and not a factor in his acceptance of me.

Trust is giving someone the freedom and responsibility to fail in order to grow. Encouragement is a process that helps us grow by giving us trust beyond our competence. To stay at our level of proven competence is to stagnate.

For me, a successful dismount from the horse was the measurement of a successful ride. For my father, mounting the horse to take my fear for a ride was the measurement of my success. Once I got on the horse, I could not fail in his eyes. This kind of trust and encouragement is what enabled me to do it. My father knew that I was afraid. But he also knew that the only way to master my fear was to take responsibility for facing it.

The difference between a father and a track-and-field coach becomes clear. The coach motivates by rewarding achievement. The outcome of a game or track meet is the standard by which success or failure is measured. By such standards, a horseback rider would be disqualified if she falls off the horse at the end. No points are awarded for a successful mount!

A father is more of an encourager than a motivator—or ought to be! Too often, I am afraid, fathers fall into the trap of being motivators rather than encouragers.

When a father also tries to be a coach, the roles and standards can become confused. A recent story in the sports pages described how the coach of a nationally ranked college basketball team kicked his son in the shins for making a bad play. The coach, who had a reputation for abusing his players as part of his motivational technique, treated his own son like a player.

The power of encouragement is measured by the degree of self-confidence it gives children to approach tasks or decisions beyond their known competence. There are two types of encouragement: the first involves *implied* confidence, and the second is a direct expression of confidence.

I have alluded to my father's implied confidence in me, demonstrated through daily routines in which he drew me in as a partner. Such implied confidence is absolutely necessary for the development of self-confidence, and it comes when those we trust demonstrate trust in us. Direct expressions of confidence ("Ray can do it") are most meaningful and inspiring when they come from a person who has already demonstrated trust in us. You cannot inspire confidence to face a new situation simply by telling someone you barely know that you trust them.

I had a fair amount of self-confidence around the horses with whom I worked and played every day. This was based on the fact that I had ridden them all and knew them. This level of confidence, however, was of no help in facing the fear produced by Wally's horse. It didn't provide the courage I needed to mount a horse with unknown power to hurt me.

Nor would I have been encouraged in the same way if Wally's father had said, "Why don't you try to ride the horse?" He didn't know me and had no reason to believe I could do it. And I had no reason to trust his judgment.

No, that would not be the same. Hidden in such explicit words of confidence is a dare. "I dare you to do it," is the implicit taunt lurking in many attempts to exhort us to face our fears. It won't work. If it does succeed in forcing us to make the attempt, the result is not the same. If we fail, it only serves to humiliate and disempower us. And if we should succeed, the success is good for only the one ride.

My father was not a daring man, by some standards. In fact, he probably was overly cautious when it came to taking risks. The only piece of land he ever bought was purchased just before the Great Depression in the 1930s. With two or three years of crop failures in a row, no payments could be made and the title reverted to the bank. Years later, he admitted that he should have taken the risk again when the prospects looked better.

There were others who were more daring, but none with the power of encouragement that he possessed—the power that came from a lifetime of implied confidence in me. This is the legacy he left with me: "Ray can do it." How many times, when faced with some challenge or unexplored option, have I heard the echo of those words! I am thankful for the one time that they were uttered—even though they were not even directed at me! And I am also thankful for the unexpressed but implied confidence that made my father loom larger than the horse and gave me the courage to mount.

COURAGE ALWAYS HAS FEAR AS A RIDING PARTNER

I said this earlier, but let me say it again. Having the courage to mount was not done in the face of fear of horses in general, but of that particular horse. When fear is generalized, it becomes more of a phobia, such as fear of flying, fear of crowds, or fear of the dark. I am speaking of a particular and specifically targeted fear. My self-confidence in riding horses was not a sufficient buffer against that fear. I needed courage in addition to self-confidence.

Courage is not the absence of fear—that may be foolhardiness. Rather, courage is the capacity to risk security and safety in order to accomplish a task that has some perceived value to the self. In the case of riding the horse, the value was directly related to how I wanted to be perceived by my father.

I had no desire and no need to ride that horse. Therefore I did not have courage to attempt it. The courage to ride came with the encouragement from my father. Fear rode with me, but it was no longer an irrational or paralyzing fear. The fear was under control, even though the horse was not!

My father's encouragement has served me well in the years since that experience. There is always some particular fear related to specific things I do—sometimes regularly, like speaking in public, or sometimes daily, like facing each new day's unknown possibilities. I don't mind this kind of fear. It seems reasonable and rational to take such risks. Courage is not measured by how great a risk or fear one takes; rather, it is measured by the degree of self-confidence one has as a result of the encouragement of others.

I realize that I have interpreted what my father said far beyond what he probably intended. But this is precisely my point. We always interpret critical experiences in a way that goes far beyond what was intended at the time. Self-confidence, or lack of it, is the result of such interpretations.

What is important is not that we conquer every fear but that we receive the encouragement to face our fears with confidence. What is important is to have experienced trust and encourage-

chapter two

ment so that when someone suddenly says "Ray can do it," you already have one leg up and are raring to go!

Finding a solution rather than fixing blame

"This is as good a time as any to learn."

With that, my father set me up on the iron seat of a plow hitched behind six horses, strung out in two teams of three each. There were three lead horses and three immediately behind them. They were controlled by two sets of leather reins, one set going to the outside horses in the lead team and the other going to the outside horses in the team behind. The middle horses had no choice but to go where the others went.

The occasion was prompted by my question about how the horses knew where to go when they came to the end of the field. I could understand them walking in a straight line as one of the lead horses walked in the freshly plowed furrow left by the previous pass down the field.

First, my father took me with him as he made a round up and down the field. Placing the reins in my small hands—I could have been no more than thirteen at the time—he let me feel the gentle pull of the horses and guided me as I pulled the proper reins to turn them in order to begin the trip back. It looked so simple with his hands guiding mine. It was as though the horses felt his familiar, firm grasp and allowed themselves to be guided smoothly around the turn.

The trick seemed to be knowing which of the four reins to

pull at the proper moment while, at the same time, keeping the other three firmly in one's hand. As I was to discover, it was more than a trick, it was an art!

One can feel only pity for those who have never sat on a horse-drawn plow, with the metal wheels jolting along the rutted ground and the smooth plowshares biting deeply into the soil. There is nothing like the sweet smell of freshly turned earth flowing like a ribbon of black water behind the plow. The only sound is the screech of sea gulls darting after worms.

The effect was hypnotic and slightly intoxicating. As the horses plodded ahead, I felt the rhythm of their movements through the reins. My fingers ached with the strain of holding the heaving leather reins so as to keep them separated and yet maintain the proper tension on each. But this was sweet agony!

It would be nice if life could be an extension of such moments. The exhilaration was exceeded only by the sense of peace and completeness. One felt connected to earth and sky by a life force that probed every one of the senses.

But life is not like that, of course. There is always a corner to be turned. And suddenly, there we were, within feet of the field's end. Now something I had not anticipated demanded attention. Just before making the turn, I had to lift the plowshares out of the ground. This was a maneuver that required the use of one foot and one hand simultaneously to operate two levers. The plow's forward movement would provide the lifting force. If I stopped the horses, the lifting power would be lost and there would be no hope of getting the shares out of the ground.

I was able to manage the tricky maneuver, but, in order to free one hand, I had to shift the reins into the other—thereby losing track of which reins went to which horse.

What happened next would have to be seen to be appreciated. In attempting to navigate the horses around the turn, I pulled on the wrong reins and the three lead horses ended up facing the three horses that followed in a tangled mess. Never before or since have I seen such a look of absolute bewilderment on the face of a horse!

It was my good fortune that they were so stunned by this turn of events that they made no attempt to disentangle themselves. Instead, they simply stood staring at each other, as if wondering who had called this meeting!

My father had already begun the long walk from the other end of the field to the scene of my disaster. That was the longest, slowest walk I have ever witnessed—not because of my father's pace, but because of my anxiety about what would happen when he arrived. There is no torture quite like stewing in the juice of one's own humiliation.

"I think I forgot to warn you about the lift," were the first words out of his mouth. The ones that followed were what made this event so significant in my life.

"What you do in this situation—and I have been in it myself—is to unhitch the horses from the plow before doing anything else. You line them up again in proper order, then hitch them up to the plow, and they will work as good as new!"

Instead of taking the job away from me, my father helped as I took responsibility to straighten out the mess I'd made. I knew about hitching up horses, I had done it for my father a hundred times. As I unhitched and then rehitched the teams, it seemed so easy. The process took some time, but by doing what I knew how to do I could begin to fix the problem caused by what I did not know how to do!

"You can always find the solution to your own problems," he commented after everything was restored to order. "After all, that comes with the job. It is more difficult to solve other people's problems." And this man never completed the eighth grade!

chapter three

✈ NO ONE TO BLAME BUT YOURSELF?

How often haven't we heard, "You have no one to blame but yourself"? That is one of the most destructive statements one could make. Why should there be a need for blame if a person takes responsibility for working out a solution?

I don't know why I expected to be blamed, because this was not typical of my father. In this case, it might be because I felt I deserved it. And I have discovered that we are more prone to blame than to excuse ourselves.

In his offhand way, my father shifted my focus from the issue of blame by taking some of the responsibility himself: "I think I forgot to warn you about the lift." Well, that was certainly not the whole problem! But it helped to have him suggest that this oversight was what precipitated the mess I got myself into.

The most important thing he did was to treat the situation as a problem to be solved rather than finding someone to blame. As far as I could tell, my father did not even blame himself for sending a young boy on such a precarious mission. "I have been in this situation myself," he said. And then he showed me how I could begin to solve the problem by drawing on what I already knew how to do.

Blaming oneself is probably one of the most common pitfalls in life. I use "blame" in this context as the opposite of taking responsibility for one's actions. When we blame ourselves or others, we are making what is only a problem into a personal failure. The hidden word in the concept of blame is "failure." And hidden in the word failure is "shame."

Blaming is a shaming tactic. When we blame others we are exposing their failure. This is a shaming act. When we blame ourselves, we are doing what we have been taught to do by a shame-based family or culture. "Taking the blame" can be a way of atoning for a mistake: we allow ourselves to be humiliated as a kind of peace offering to those who judge us.

There is often a spiritual dimension to "taking the blame," as though God will be appeased by our shame and humiliation. People who feel shame when they experience failure believe in a shaming god. Instead of receiving forgiveness for a wrong, they offer their shame as a form of penance. The god who blames is the god who shames.

"You ought to be ashamed of yourself" comes so easily to our lips when someone does something offensive or inappropriate. If the person did feel ashamed, does that mean that the offense is somehow less offensive? Or does it mean that, because shame robs us of virtue and value, it is the price we must pay to be forgiven? If so, such forgiveness is shame-based, leaving the forgiven person weak and wounded rather than empowered and whole.

Whatever purpose, shame becomes toxic and crippling when it is pervasive and persistent. Blame is always shaming by its nature and disempowering in its effect. Taking responsibility may require more effort, but it is more productive and creative.

YOU CAN'T START OVER UNTIL YOU ADMIT DEFEAT!

One important lesson the incident with the plow taught me is that you better know how to hitch the horses before you take the reins. The solution to the problem was really quite simple, once my father helped me see what to do. I was trying to think of how I could drive the horses out of the tangle by using the same reins that got me into it. Because this was impossible, I was baffled. The more I would pull on the reins, the more confused the situation would become. Even the horses would be bewildered by this strategy.

Unhitching the horses and starting over never occurred to me. Perhaps it was because this would be to admit defeat. My father had suffered many defeats and had to start over. My bungled attempt at plowing followed by only two or three years the time my father borrowed money to buy land, only to have three crop failures make it impossible to make a payment. The farm reverted to the bank, and he had to "unhitch the horses" as it were, and start over.

Did my father blame himself for losing what little money he had in the down payment? I doubt it. If so, there was never any evidence. A man who frequently blames himself would be the first to blame his son. Blame is passed on from parents to children, and it becomes a way of life.

On the other hand, the acceptance of failure without self-blame begins the creative process of problem solving. I gained more competence in learning how to solve the problem I had created than if I had managed by good luck and the help of angels to successfully turn the corner.

The Great Depression of the 1930s did not cause massive psychological depression among farmers. Bad luck and crop failure were not seen as measures of personal worth; rather, they became a challenge to survive by "unhitching" and starting over. Few farmers blamed themselves for what they could not control, and even fewer blamed God.

Taking responsibility for one's life and one's failures is not to deny the role of God in life. I have no trouble with a God who admits that humans were placed in a dangerous world with little skill to navigate life's treacherous corners. I have more difficulty with a God who would take over completely and not show me how to take responsibility for my actions.

TAKING RESPONSIBILITY MEANS STOP BLAMING

As I reflect on the effect this experience had on me, I discover several things that have made a difference in my life.

First: blame doesn't solve problems. I grew up with little need to blame myself or others. I have made my share of mistakes. Some of these I could solve by unhitching and starting over, and some I simply had to let fall by the wayside as problems that I couldn't solve. Today when I hear farmers use the expression "crop failure" rather than "farming failure," I recall the important lessons my father taught me about avoiding blame.

Second: taking responsibility for our failures is the first step toward success. Blaming others for our own failures is an indication that we have not yet assumed responsibility. We are blaming others to excuse our own failure and as a way of easing the pain caused by self-blame.

My father took part of the responsibility for the problem with the plow: he admitted that he had failed to train me sufficiently for the task. But he did not take on my responsibility for learning how to solve my own problem. When I had rehitched the horses and turned the corner, I felt that my first experience at plowing was a success.

Third: starting over is often the best way to overcome defeat. I knew something about hitching horses before I tried to drive them. The solution to the problem of the tangled reins was well within the expertise of a thirteen-year-old boy who had performed this chore many times. It did not occur to me to unhitch the horses and start over because this seemed like admitting defeat. Although I did not have enough expertise to turn the corner, I had the necessary competence to untangle the horses and start over.

In a figurative sense, we all learn how to hitch horses before we learn how to drive them. This means that some of the solutions to our adult problems may well lie with the expertise we gained when we were younger. Why do we need someone to tell us that?

Fourth: it is not a weakness to accept help from others.

chapter three

Having someone else step in to help you clean up your mess may seem humiliating. I learned from my father that it need not be. Today when I overreach my ability or misjudge my competence, or simply flat out make a silly mistake, I look for people who know more than I do in order to get the plow back in the ground again.

I was trained as a navigator during my stint with the Army Air Force in the Second World War. On one training mission, I was to provide the navigation for a three-hour flight from an air base in Texas out over the Gulf of Mexico and back. The coordinates were given to me, and I was to direct the pilot solely by using celestial navigation, with no radio communication.

Well out over the Gulf of Mexico, I told the pilot to take a new heading, based on my calculations, that should take us back to the air base. In a few minutes, he called back to me, "By my reckoning we'll hit the east coast of South America before we hit Texas if I follow your heading!" I was stunned and mortified. What had gone wrong?

The pilot offered to give me five minutes to find my error. If I couldn't, he would use the radio to get the correct heading. It was no use. Despite the pages of calculations based on my sextant reading of the sun and my charts, I was stumped. Looking out of the window I saw nothing but water. Once again I had tangled the horses, and the only thing to do was to "unhitch" and start over. I called the pilot and told him as much, asking him to use the radio to get us home.

It was a long flight back—similar to waiting for my father to walk the length of that field long ago. When we landed, my instructor came up to me and said, "Now you know what it is to be lost, and now you know how to depend on others. We don't trust navigators who haven't been lost and asked for help!"

"This is as good a time as any to learn," my father had said when he put me behind the plow for the first time. He thought he was going to teach me to plow. And he did. But in the plowing lesson, I learned far more than he intended. I learned to take responsibility for my actions in a positive way. I learned how to accept help from others. And, most of all, I learned not to fix blame but to move toward solutions. Those are lessons that I need to apply every day of my life.

It is easier to do it right the first time

he smell of freshly cut grass flowing behind the sickle bar of a horse-drawn mower is caught by the breeze and sweetens the warm July air. It is haying season. At the age of fifteen, I am old enough to mow the field in preparation for the curing and stacking process. By now, well accustomed to handling horses, I approach the task with relish.

The clatter of the mower as it slices through wind-blown grass over a foot tall is musical accompaniment to the performance. Round and round the field I drive the horses, careful to keep them from crowding over too far so that a strip of grass is left uncut. But not careful enough, as it turns out!

Turning corners requires dexterity and timing. Reining the horses sharply around a ninety-degree angle, the mower bar is lifted with a foot lever so as not to catch and clog in the cut grass. The idea is to begin cutting a new swath, leaving a nice square corner.

I'm pretty good at it, but not perfect. My timing is not always accurate, and the mower bar drags some cut grass into the uncut portion, leaving a patch standing. At times, the horses are preoccupied with their own thoughts and do not respond as quickly as I would like. As a result, many of the corners look a little ragged.

When I am through, the field is basically mown. However, strips of still-standing grass here and there, and patches of uncut grass at the corners, stand as incriminating evidence of my carelessness coupled with lack of skill.

As my father surveys the scene, I have a sinking feeling. "Good enough" is not a concept that he has chosen as a philosophy of life.

"Well, son," he says slowly, "you got most of it the first time, but you're not finished yet. Now if you go back out there a second time, you can get the rest."

With that, I turn the horses back and head for the uncut strips and patches at the corners. What once worked so smoothly is now a nightmare. Every time I lower the blade with the foot lever to cut the small uncut strips, the mower catches the cut grass and clogs. I back the horses up and try it again. Even the horses begin to look around to see what madness is causing this wretched stopping and starting.

Finally I give up and bring the mower home.

"It's impossible, Dad," I protest. "The cut grass clogs the mower, and I can't cut the small strips and patches."

"Yes," he responded, "I know that from experience. That's why it is easier to do it right the first time."

Is there no end to my father's lessons in life?

✈ No Excuse, Sir!

Was my dad being unfair? After all, I was young and lacked necessary experience to perform the task with the precision and skill required. Lack of experience ought to excuse what a more proficient mower would call sloppy work. I could have offered excuses for not doing the job well, but my father was not interested in excuses. I did not need him to tell me what a ragged job I had done. The evidence was there for all to see: forlorn patches of uncut grass bowed as though embarrassed to be left standing amidst their fallen comrades.

At the same time, I did not feel scolded or shamed by his response. He simply said that the job was not finished. He was not judging me according to his own standards, nor did he make me feel a failure. The scattered patches of uncut grass were really quite insignificant: no cows would go hungry that winter because of my inexperienced mowing. What difference did it make, then?

Just this: the mowing of the field had also to do with the growing of a boy. I had done a fairly good job, under the circumstances. But even *I* knew that it was not good enough. My father could have excused me, saying that it was pretty good for the first time, thereby teaching me that excuses can absolve one of responsibility for sloppy work.

By sending me out to mow the field a second time, he gave me ownership of the task. I was not allowed to excuse myself for a poor job simply because I lacked the skill and experience. He could have mown the field himself or hired an experienced man to do it if his main concern was getting a perfect job. In asking me to do the work, my father gave me responsibility for it. No matter how it turned out, it was my work. No excuses!

In the end, the ragged field was left as it was; no further efforts were made toward a perfect job. The next time I mowed, however, I gave far greater attention to the task, remembering how difficult it was to go over it a second time!

Years later, during basic training in the Army Air Force, when summoned before an officer to give an account of some infraction, I was told that the only acceptable response was, "No excuse, sir!" I will not reveal how many times I had to utter those words, but I had no difficulty saying them. I had learned from my father that there may be a reason for failing, but an excuse is not a reason!

The reasons that I could not mow the field skillfully were my youth and my inexperience. They could not, however, be excuses for accepting sloppy work. Getting something right the first time became the motto and standard by which I approached all future tasks of life.

✺ WHEN MAKING EXCUSES BECOMES A HABIT

Making excuses can become a habit. The phrase "excuse me" slips into our culture and becomes a standard of etiquette as well as a moral convenience. To excuse yourself when bumping into someone in a crowd is an expected social grace. To excuse an act of violence as a "crime of passion" is to absolve a person of responsibility and to mitigate punishment.

While I was living in Scotland during two years of graduate study, I learned that instead of saying "excuse me" when jostling another in a crowd, the proper response was "Sorry!" In an effort to fit into the culture, I quickly learned the custom. I suppose the effect of both expressions is much the same. Yet there is a significant difference between saying "excuse me" and "I am sorry."

The first expression places the responsibility on the offended person: "Excuse me, I did not intend to intrude upon your space." The second acknowledges personal wrongdoing and places the responsibility on the offender—leaving the offended person free to forgive or not. "I am sorry. I stepped on your foot, and I take responsibility for it."

It is not hard to see why making excuses can easily become a habit. The first instinct on being caught in some violation or personal failure is to find an excuse. One can either seek to be excused from blame by pleading special circumstances or projecting the blame on another party.

"Excuse me, officer, but I have never driven in this part of town before. I did not realize that this was a one-way street."

Or, "Excuse me for being late with this report. My husband crashed the computer, and I spent all day yesterday getting the hard disk operating again."

chapter four

Excuse making has a long history.

In the biblical account of the first humans, the man and woman were given a task—to care for the earth—and a command—not to eat of one tree in the garden God had given them. By eating fruit from the tree of the knowledge of good and evil, they violated the command, and they fled from the face of God. When God called them forth and asked for an accounting, the man cast blame: "The woman you gave to be with me, she gave me fruit from the tree, and I ate." On her part, the woman said, "The serpent tricked me, and I ate." The serpent said not a word but, given a human nature, it no doubt would have responded, "The devil made me do it!"

We make excuses for a number of reasons: to avoid punishment, to soften the blow of failure, and to escape the consequences of our commitments.

The New Testament Gospel of Luke describes how Jesus responded to some people who had expressed interest in becoming his followers. He told a parable about a man who gave a great dinner and invited many guests. But when pressed for their acceptance, "they all alike began to make excuses." One said that he could not come because he had bought a piece of land, another excused himself because he had purchased five yoke of oxen, and yet another bowed out because he had just been married. To his would-be followers, Jesus explained: "No one who puts his hand to the plow and looks back is fit for the kingdom of God."

The making of excuses has become our way of life. It is reinforced through well-meaning attempts by our caretakers to ease the pain of failure and to gloss over the horror of senseless violence.

The excuse "boys will be boys" was recently offered by a mother whose teenage son was killed by three other teenagers in a school-ground brawl. The newspaper reported her comment in a story that noted her lack of anger and spirit of forgiveness toward those who murdered her son. When one cannot find a reason for senseless violence, one often offers such excuses in an attempt to preserve a sense of sanity.

A bloody urban riot is excused as an authentic rebellion against the tyranny of economic and racial oppression. No matter that innocent persons are killed and the property of many is destroyed. Children who murder their parents are often excused as innocent victims of abuse, their brutal act made somehow acceptable and, the defense argues, necessary in order to right a greater wrong.

But these are "extraordinary" incidents, far removed from the daily lives of most of us. We would likely excuse ourselves from being considered in the same category as "these people." Do you see now how the habit of excusing serves to distance us from that which we condemn?

While we deplore the outrageous use of excuses for wanton acts of violence, we are quite comfortable with the practical value of excuses that smooth the ragged edges of broken promises and provide a safe retreat from sometimes heroic demands of duty.

"Doing it right the first time" doesn't mean that our first efforts must be perfect, but that we assume responsibility for seeing that the task is done right—and we won't be satisfied until it is. People who use excuses to avoid taking such responsibility tend to find refuge in roles: "I'm just a boy"; "I was an innocent bystander"; "I've only worked here for three months." Roles can be impersonal and safe, and they provide a good excuse for avoiding personal involvement.

"You are not finished yet," was my father's judgment. The fact that I was just a boy was not an excuse for sloppy work. When I was given the task, it was not an experiment to see how good I was. It was an opportunity for me to learn responsibility for the quality of my work, and thus for the integrity of my life. My self-esteem was enhanced more by being treated as an equal than by being excused because I was only a child.

Suppose my father had excused my work by saying, "You did the best you could for someone of your age and experience. You did as well as I expected." On the one hand, I would have felt pleased by his affirmation. Being young and inexperienced meant that I was not held to the same standard as he was. I could go back to my toys and make believe I was farming!

On the other hand, I would have known that I did not do a good job. I would have felt like a failure by my own standards, for I knew what good mowing was. Being excused because of my youth and inexperience would have separated me from the adult world into which I was moving. Several repetitions of this kind of experience easily could have created a pattern of using excuses to cover the gap between standards and performance.

When someone offers an excuse for us, we may interpret our performance as better than it was, even though we have not met the standard. Being excused sends a message that we are no longer responsible for our actions. Children who are not held accountable become adults who use excuses to avoid responsibility for their actions—adults who have a pattern of failures to meet deadlines, perform tasks correctly, and keep promises faithfully.

The paradox is that, by using excuses to avoid being charged with failure, we develop patterns of failure throughout our life!

🏹 BREAKING THE HABIT OF MAKING EXCUSES

How can we get out of the habit of using excuses to cover for sloppy work?

First, we can take responsibility for solving a problem rather than use the problem as an excuse to stop working. Being raised on a farm, I acquired a knack for fixing things when they were broken. Most farm machinery could be fixed by using a few simple tools, a bit of common sense (if somebody put this thing together, there must be a way to take it apart!), and a willingness to get your hands dirty.

When a harvesting operation stopped because of machinery breakdown, the hired hands headed for the shade. The breakdown was an excuse for a rest and maybe a short nap. For my father, of course, this was not a time for excuses. It was his farm, his harvest. He had to solve the problem. I can remember getting right in there with him—probably more of a nuisance than a help—to solve the problem.

This problem-solving attitude has gotten me into trouble on more than one occasion. Later in life, I ended up as a hired hand, so to speak, on the faculty of a school. When problems arose at the administrative level or with the curriculum, I looked for solutions. When confronted with an organizational system where the persons with responsibility excused themselves from fixing what was broken, I instinctively got my toolbox out. I discovered that organizational bureaucracy is often an excuse for inefficient job performance.

By sending me back to correct my sloppy job of mowing, my father taught me that the only real failure is not dealing with problems that we're responsible for solving. Many things that we call failures and make excuses for are, in fact, merely problems that we are responsible for solving.

Think how this attitude would affect our relationships in marriage, family, and friendship. When we don't assume responsibility for our problems, they often become failures for which we create excuses.

Second, we can stop making excuses by accepting the consequence of having no excuse. I first learned what "No excuse, sir" meant in a barracks inspection during basic training. When the inspecting officer discovered a shirt in my wardrobe with the sleeves unbuttoned, he lectured me and assigned a demerit. I tried to explain that a friend had borrowed the shirt and returned it unbuttoned.

"I am not interested in how it happened," the officer said. "The correct answer is 'No excuse, sir!' " That demerit was added to a list of other minor infractions he discovered, and I was confined to barracks the following weekend.

The consequence of having no excuse was painful because I felt that it had not been my fault. But it wasn't any help to blame my friend. Losing a friend was a further consequence that I was not prepared to suffer!

In the future, I prepared for the inspections by double-checking everything, never again assuming that a friend would "do it right the first time." It is amazing how many things work better when approached with the attitude that no excuse will be accepted if it is not done right.

I receive a variety of excuses from students who turn papers in late or who plead special consideration for sloppy work or unfinished projects. The computer, I have found, has become the student's best friend when it comes to excusing unfinished course work. It is surprising how many computers develop problems the night before a major paper is due!

One student amazed me by attaching a note to his week-late paper, saying he would understand if I didn't accept it and gave him a failing grade for the course. "I simply have no excuse," he wrote.

The fact that this kind of response is so rare says a great deal about the excuse-making nature of our society.

Third, we can break the habit of using excuses if we live by grace rather than by law. Making excuses is actually a very legalistic approach to life. If our excuses are accepted, we feel acquitted of wrongdoing. By offering excuses, we are saying that we should not be held responsible for our action or lack of action.

This will seem surprising to some. Excusing people from responsibility for their mistakes or wrongdoings is often thought to be a form of grace, because it seems to release them from consequences. However, in being excused, we are also paying a price.

If my father had excused me from further responsibility concerning the sloppy mowing, it would have been at the cost of my participation in his adult world. My intention had been to undertake a responsibility that was perhaps beyond my years, but it was one that I had every intention of growing into. I was moving out of the world of children's games into the world of adult reality.

When my father did not provide an excuse for me, but sent me back out to finish the job, he was in effect saying, "Your work counts and has value, so you must give it your best." By affirming my partnership in his world and giving me ownership of the task, he exposed me to a possible performance failure but not to a personal failure. What counted was that I was given the dignity, freedom, and responsibility of having a task by which I could take my place in his world, the real world of adults. This was my father's gift to me. This was living by grace.

To further explore this idea of grace, I'll briefly return to the first recorded examples of excuses—the ones offered to God in the biblical account of Adam and Eve. When they offered excuses for eating the forbidden fruit, the Lord refused to accept them. God would not absolve them of responsibility because they were participants with God in the world he had created. The Genesis account of creation says that people were given the very image and likeness of God: therefore they certainly could not be excused for disobeying God's command. There would be consequences for their actions. And once they had owned up to their responsibility, their guilt, they would be ready to accept God's grace and forgiveness.

Forgiveness is never the granting of an excuse, for in that

case, there is nothing to forgive. Real forgiveness—which is a gift, which is grace—says, "Your life counts and I send you forth to finish the job!"

The New Testament Gospel of John describes this kind of grace in Jesus' words to his closest followers (who had turned a lot of sloppy corners in their attempt to harvest fruit for the kingdom of God): "I do not call you servants any longer, because the servant does not know what the master is doing: but I have called you friends, because I have made known to you everything that I have heard from my Father" (John 15:15).

These are words of forgiveness for failure. This is an invitation to partnership and responsibility—no excuses allowed! This is grace.

The day that I made such a miserable mess of the mowing job, I truly began to be a partner with, a follower of, my father. Years later, I drew on that experience to understand what it means to become a follower of God. God's followers are God's partners, and no excuses are permitted between partners!

Putting your faith in the seed and not in the harvest

t was Saturday evening and harvesttime. I was but a young boy, and had to stretch my legs to match my father's stride as we walked out into the barley field. The ripening grain flowed almost to my father's waist and to my shoulders as we waded into this river of gold.

"It's about ready," my father said, as much to himself as to me. "Come Monday we will begin cutting."

I don't know what his dreams were that night, but mine were of the excitement of following the horse-drawn harvester around the field, watching the bundles spew out, each tied with rough twine by the clicking fingers of the mechanical apparatus. My job was to stack them into shocks with the grain ends on top, a bearded bouquet of sunlit straw.

But my dreams did not come true. On Sunday afternoon, a thunderstorm marched across the prairie, stabbing the ground with lightning and pelting all within its stride with merciless hailstones. The frozen ice pellets drove animals under cover, tore shingles off the roof, and cut the standing grain to a mangled, broken straw.

When the storm had passed, we walked once more out into the field. My father surveyed the sodden wreckage with eyes as practiced in measuring chaos as in envisioning a harvest. When he spoke, it was directly to me, as though he were depositing the words, like seeds, into a freshly plowed field.

"Son, when this field dries out, we will begin to work it to keep the weeds down. A fall rain is good for the subsoil. We still have seed for planting in the spring, and it will grow a better crop next year for all of this."

This was surely not his first crop loss, nor would it be his last. I have often wondered how he felt at the time. If he expressed any anger or bitterness, it was beyond my capacity to perceive. This I remember: there was no cursing of the earth and no angry gesture toward heaven. There was no apparent self-recrimination for failing to start the harvest earlier.

Psychologists might have considered this lack of any outrage unhealthy. Better to express anger than to repress and internalize feelings of grief and disappointment. My father, they would have assured me, was a typical inexpressive male. I doubt it! Never has a person communicated more depth of feeling and capacity for faith than my father expressed in his words to me.

Misfortune had struck. And my father struck back in the only way he knew how. He wagered the power of new seed against the destructive fury of that storm. By the time we had returned to the house that Sunday evening, he had decided which crop he would plant in that field. My father had not lost hope, only a harvest. His thoughts were already on the coming spring and planting season.

We can have strong feelings only for that which has the capacity to break our hearts. We can only mend a broken heart by sowing the seeds for a future harvest. He loved the soil and the seed more than the harvest! This is the lesson hope teaches us.

     🖋 THOSE WHO LIVE FOR THE HARVEST MAY
         DIE BY THE HARVEST

In my youth I was more fascinated with harvesttime than planting time. Early spring days seemed bleak and planting

chores were drudgery. Nor did summer stir my soul: caring for
the crops during sweltering South Dakota summers was a constant battle against weeds, insects, and the worrisome weather.
My eager hopes were fixed on the harvest.

In my youth and inexperience, I saw the barley harvest as the
only thing that counted. When devastation struck, I could not
understand how, despite the hardship and personal disappointment, it was not the collapse of my father's life investment in
farming. Not only had he learned to diversify his crops so that
the harvest season was spread out over a longer period, he had
learned to diversify his emotional investment in life. No harvest
misfortune had the power to rob him of the self-fulfillment that
came with planting time.

My father struck back by launching another season of preparing and planning. There is emotional wisdom and personal
power in taking initiative in the face of life's misfortunes. Not
every seed will produce a harvest, but the planting of seeds is a
step of faith that renews hope.

As we move out of our youth into adulthood, we begin to
experience the losses and failures that come with every new venture. The word "misfortune" captures the emotional impact of a
sudden loss. One definition of fortune is "prosperity attained
partly through luck." A good growing season and good weather
through harvest mean good fortune for the farmer. Despite the
wisdom, skill, and hard labor that go into the growing of a crop,
the harvest is largely dependent upon fortune. To lose the harvest, in the end, is unfortunate. But it need not be fatal.

At the same time, a bountiful harvest is as much good fortune as it is good husbandry of the soil. This is why the farmer's
security of soul had better not rest solely on the outcome of
the harvest.

Life is best lived from one sowing to another, not from one
harvest to another. A good harvest is a time of rejoicing and

thanksgiving at life's bounty. But if harvest is all that stirs the heart, what is left when the harvest fails?

If we're willing to pay the premium, we can insure against some of life's misfortunes. Insurance, however, does not prevent misfortune; it only serves to compensate for the material or financial loss caused by misfortune. Some farmers pay an annual premium for hail insurance on their crops. But hail is only one of the calamities that can ruin a good harvest. Too much rain at the wrong time, extended drought, plant disease, or an early frost can be just as devastating. One cannot insure against every risk that threatens the crop.

When we venture into personal relationships and undertake commitments that involve risking what we love most, we can experience losses against which there is no insurance or compensation. To lose that which we have loved and in which we have made investments of passion and effort is heartbreaking. It can lead to an empty and broken life.

Our deepest feelings are often invested in that which has the capacity to break our hearts. At the same time, it is necessary to make these risky investments in order to plant the seed of love in the soil of life. The risk of failure is no reason not to go forth and plant.

The key to all such investments is to pin our hopes on the planting and not on the harvest. If we put our faith in the seeds of love and fix our hopes on the constant renewal and promise that comes with planting, we can survive the worst disasters and harvest failures.

✤ Sowing the seeds of faith

There is no better metaphor for the expression of faith than that of sowing seed, for it requires investing ourselves in a task for which we cannot control the outcome.

We exercise the gift of faith by planting new seeds amidst disaster and ruin. My father looked out over the field where his hopes for a harvest lay in ruins and envisioned a new planting season. Faith turns to the task of planting. Hope is given new life with the sowing of seed in expectation of a new harvest.

When we sow seed in the soil, we invest our time, energy, and limited resources in the power and promise of life. This is as good a definition of faith as I know.

Those who demonstrate the unusual ability to strike back when misfortune strikes have learned to exercise the power of faith. They save some seed from every harvest to sow in the fields savaged by the cruel storms of life. These people are not exceptional saints, they are ordinary sowers who, empowered by grace, have extraordinary faith in the power and promise of life.

Edna St. Vincent Millay paints a word picture of a farmer whose land has been devastated by a flood:

The broken dike, the levee washed away,
The good fields flooded and the cattle drowned,
Estranged and treacherous all the faithful ground,
And nothing left but bloating disarray
Of tree and home uprooted,—was this the day
Man dropped upon his shadow without a sound
And died, having laboured well and having found
His burden heavier than a quilt of clay?
No, no. I saw him when the sun had set
In water, leaning on his single oar
Above his garden faintly glimmering yet . . .
There bulked the plough, here washed the updrifted weeds . . .
And scull across his roof and make for shore,
With twisted face and pocket full of seeds.

("Sonnet X" of *Epitaph for the Race of Man*,
from *Collected Poems*, edited by Norma Millay,
New York: HarperCollins, 1981, p. 710)

chapter five

An ancient Hebrew poet captured a similar philosophy of life in one of the Old Testament psalms:

May those who sow in tears reap with shouts of joy.
Those who go out weeping,
bearing the seed for sowing,
shall come home with shouts of joy,
carrying their sheaves.

Ps. 126

A literal translation of the Hebrew text reads this way:

He surely toils along weeping,
carrying the burden of seed;
he surely comes in with rejoicing,
carrying his sheaves.

What a strange phrase—"the burden of seed." Then it struck me: seeds are a burden, for they carry within them the hope of the planter. And hope can be a heavy burden indeed. At harvesttime there is rejoicing, for the hope has ripened into fruit. But planting the seed requires an exercise of faith and a burden of hope.

🦌 THE BURDEN OF HOPE

The burden of hope must be borne if we are to see new life emerge from the seed. Let me explore some ways in which it is possible to shoulder this burden.

First, the burden of hope is weighted with anguish over what has already been lost. In the poignant sonnet by Edna St. Vincent Millay, it is with "twisted face" that the man with the pocket full of seeds moves toward the future. We should never forget this. Hope always emerges out of the ruins of some failed dream, some unfulfilled desire, some loss that must be grieved.

There is a kind of hope that is childish and immature. It is short-term and short-lived. It flickers for an instant and then quickly dissolves with the first tears of frustration over loss. That hope is merely a fantasy, an illusion which shares the same bed with fear—both are ghosts in the night and cannot survive the bright light of day. True hope is not a wish or desire that can be washed away with the first summer storm.

Hope was expressed in the Bible following the first murder. Eve was the mother of two sons, Cain and Abel. After Cain had killed Abel, we read, "Adam knew his wife again, and she bore a son and called his name Seth, for she said, 'God has appointed for me another child instead of Abel, for Cain slew him'" (Gen. 4:25). I can imagine Eve whispering to herself, "Will Seth be killed also? Will I lose this son too?"

There are those who would not have risked another child, another tragic loss. There are those who prefer never to try again rather than suffer the anguish of bearing hope. This is the "twisted face" that accompanies the burden of hope.

Hope requires risk, so much risk that it hurts. Hope always makes us vulnerable to some future and even greater loss. Hope exposes us to disappointment, frustration, and betrayal. Faith plants the seed and promises a harvest, and so creates hope. But with the promise comes the possibility that the promise will fail. That is the burden that hope must bear.

Without faith in the promise and power of life, the burden of hope could not be borne. Faith enables us to bear that burden, for it is partnership with God, the author and creator of life.

Second, the burden of hope is the responsibility that attends the bearer of the seed. The one who bears the seed is not just a carrier, but a sower. Seed also can be carried in a bucket or stored in a sack. The burden of hope demands that the sower prepare the soil, plant the seed, and nurture the growth of the seed through to harvest.

The burden of hope involves responsibility for once again taking up life after failure and foolishness. The biblical parable of the prodigal son describes how a young man cut himself off from his father and foolishly squandered his inheritance before coming to his senses. When he returned home begging to be taken in as a servant, his father welcomed him with open arms—but not as a servant. The prodigal was forgiven and restored to his position as son. And with this gift, he was given a son's burden—a "pocket full of seeds," as it were—to join his brother in tending their father's fields.

When a woman was brought before Jesus disgraced and condemned for her sin of adultery, Jesus told her that he did not condemn her. Instead, he told her, "Go now, and leave your life of sin" (John 8:11). The woman's forgiveness and freedom also became a burden of hope. She may have gone away from Jesus with "twisted face and pocket full of seeds," bearing far more responsibility as a result of her forgiveness. But because Jesus forgave her, she now had a partnership with God that could enable her to bear the burden of responsibility for a new life.

Third, the burden of hope is our helplessness to care for the seed in the face of the unpredictable storms of life. Without rain the seed will not grow. But with every rain cloud there looms the possibility of a ravaging and cruel storm.

How do we care for the seeds of love when they are threatened by the destructive storms of sickness, death, jealousy, hatred, senseless violence, and betrayal? And these are forces that threaten the investments we have placed in our relationships, our goals, our very lives. How can we bear the burden of hope amidst such overwhelming odds?

Here is where the analogy of the farmer and seed takes on even more meaning. The seed has a capacity to draw what it needs from the limitless resources around it and from the power for life that lies within it—provided it is sown. Just as the storms that threaten the seed are beyond our control, so are the resources and power that will make it grow. The life-giving force that can carry a seed through to harvest comes from God.

Our task is to plant the seed and do what we can to nurture the young plant. Beyond that, the matter is in God's hands—a matter of faith.

This wisdom is instinctive to one who tills the soil, and it was a wisdom that my father acquired, not through sermons in church, but through his husbandry of the soil.

As I look back upon my father's remarkable capacity to look beyond the ruined harvest to a new planting season on that very field, I think that I can discern the quiet discipline of faith. He maintained a sense of self-identity and self-worth through the diligence, faithfulness, and hope with which he persevered in his vocation. His life was that of one who cared for the soil, the seed, and his livestock.

He exercised faith by finding self-worth in his role as a planter, not merely a harvester. He bore the burden of the seed by caring for that which was an extension of his life. The fortunes of the harvest lay outside his control. A ruined harvest was a loss to be felt and grieved. But it was not a judgment against his life or his worth. The crops may fail, but not the one who cares for them.

The discipline of faith begins with caring for that which contributes to our sense of integrity, dignity, and self-worth. Refusing to blame oneself or others for misfortune begins by not taking credit for that which is in God's hands. The task that faces us all is to invest our life, through faith, in hope again and again after disaster strikes.

My father's net worth was not very much from a financial standpoint. The ruined barley harvest was but one of many misfortunes that befell him. But his personal net worth grew steadily as he exercised faith, practiced good husbandry, and accumulated treasure for himself in heaven. When disasters struck, he

chapter five

struck back through the investment of his life in a ritual of preparing the soil and planting the seed. This is the gift of a grace-empowered life, and God is the giver.

chapter six

Living by your convictions, even when they are costly

ver the rumble and roar of its engine, a threshing machine spews golden grain out of its side and belches bright yellow straw out of its back, creating a huge fluffy mountain in the farmyard. Even the most experienced farmer will admit the thrill and splendor of such a sight. This is the culmination of the harvest season. The mound of straw will provide an inexhaustible resource for bedding the farm animals during the winter, and a cozy refuge for the tiny wild creatures who will burrow in to escape the cold winds.

What matters most, of course, is the precious grain: some to be stored for feed, and some to be sold for cash to pay the bills that have accumulated. Even the merchants in town have a stake in the enterprise, for now they can expect payment on long-overdue accounts.

I was seventeen years old, in my last year of high school, and it was my task to drive the horse-drawn wagon full of grain and scoop the contents into the granary. Except for the ancient tractor that drives the threshing machine, the entire operation is dependent upon horsepower. Teams of horses hitched to large, four-wheel racks go to and fro from the nearby fields. Pulling the empty wagons from thresher to field, the horses move in a trot. Returning, they move slowly, laboring to pull the wagons stacked high with grain.

chapter six

Drawing up to the gaping, chain-driven feeder, the horses patiently wait with half-closed eyes amidst the blowing dust and chaff. One by one, the bundles are thrown into the machine to be devoured by the slashing knives and mysterious innards of the contraption. Miraculously—even to this seventeen-year-old "veteran"—the shuddering, shaking monster cleanly separates straw and chaff from the grain.

From morning to dusk, the operation continues, with only a brief shutdown at noon while men and boys troop to the farmhouse for dinner: a spread of fried chicken, roasted ears of sweet corn, mashed potatoes, gravy, and heaps of homemade bread, washed down with coffee poured from a two-gallon pot on the wood-burning stove. Morning and afternoon lunches are provided at the threshing site. Men take turns wolfing down sandwiches washed down with swigs of coffee from glass jars that will be used for canning fruit and vegetables later in the fall.

These brief respites in the shade of a rack piled with bundles are anticipated with relish, and terminated reluctantly. Break time is also story time. Tales are told of the olden days—anecdotes that bring to life people who were long dead but whose names have lived on. In this rural community, everyone is inducted into the hall of fame through such storytelling. Young boys creep close, snitch a sandwich or a piece of cake, and pretend to be men: hanging on every word, laughing too loudly and too soon, pretending a worldly wisdom, nodding in agreement with an observation it took their grandfathers fifty years to understand.

There is another ritual on mornings of threshing days. While the horses are being hitched to the wagons and the threshing machine receives new applications of oil and grease, my father and the owner of the threshing rig take turns twisting handfuls of straw in their hands and looking at the sky. Today, people viewing this scene from the vantage point of fifty years and computer-driven technology might well conclude that this was some primitive religious rite, invoking or placating the deity of the harvest.

But they would be wrong. This was a crude but quite accurate estimate of the straw's moisture content. The overnight dew turns the brittle straw into sodden stalks so that it is impossible to separate the grain from the chaff. When the morning sun has warmed the earth and evaporated the dew from the straw, the threshing can begin. But only then. Sometimes an hour or two will pass, with each worker finding a way to occupy the time until the signal is given. Then the roar of the tractor sounds the beginning of the day's work.

There is also an evening ritual. As the sun goes down, the owner of the threshing rig makes regular visits to the back of the machine. Sticking his hand into a cavity where threshed straw passes into the blower, he pulls out a handful. Examining it carefully, he looks for unthreshed heads of grain, indicating that the moisture content is rising in the cool of the evening. His word is law. When he cries "Shut it down!" the workers stop pitching the bundles into the machine. In a few minutes, all is quiet. The horses are unhitched, the last load of grain is scooped into the granary, and man and beast find sustenance in cool water, ample food, and the quiet solace of a moonlit night.

This glimpse of a nearly forgotten craft and culture may well be something that I needed to share more than you, the reader, needed to know. I do not deny a certain nostalgic self-indulgence in telling this. But what I am about to say can be understood best only in the light of those long-ago days.

Some truths cannot be told without a story. And there are timeless truths that are embedded in the fabric of people's lives beyond the time and place in which they live. This is one of those truths.

✈ THE COSTLINESS OF CONVICTIONS

It was Saturday evening. The owner of the threshing rig approached my father after calling for the operation to stop. The straw was getting too wet, the grain was not being threshed.

"We were almost done," he said as if in disbelief. "There are only two racks of bundles to be threshed. It's a pity that we couldn't have finished so our crew could be on its way to the next job."

"No matter," my father said, "there's always another day."

"That's what I was going to suggest," the rig owner said. "We will start up first thing in the morning, knock out those two loads of bundles, and be on our way."

"But tomorrow is Sunday," my father said. "We don't work on Sunday. We will wait until Monday morning and then finish."

"Don't be a fool," the owner replied. "These horses will eat more oats over the weekend than the two racks of bundles contain! It doesn't make sense to feed the horses and the men over Sunday just for two loads. Think about the cost! Surely you can make an exception in this case."

"I'm sorry," my father replied, "but I have never had to work on Sunday to get my work done, and I am not about to start now."

With that, the incident was over. I have no clear recollection of that Sunday or the following Monday. I suppose that we did the chores as usual on Sunday morning and then went to church, and that the threshing was finished on Monday.

I doubt that my father knew I was close enough to overhear his conversation with the owner of the rig. He never mentioned it afterward, and, to my knowledge, never gave any of us an explanation as to why he did not work on Sunday. He just didn't. That was no doubt one way in which he lived out his faith. The Lutheran tradition in which he was raised was not noted for being legalistic or demanding about such things as attending church or observing Sundays. My father's observance of Sunday worship was most likely rooted in his personal convictions.

Convictions can be costly. But until our beliefs have been tested, they mean very little. As a boy, I stood by my father's side in church Sunday after Sunday while we recited the creed, our statement of faith about the God in whom we believed. I listened as my father recited words that pledged his faith and trust in God. But it was the firm expression of his conviction not to thresh two loads of grain on a Sunday that made an indelible impression on me.

Convictions have a certain nobility about them. We tend to respect people of conviction. There are many people who hold deep convictions and pay a high price for them. But conviction itself is not enough. People sometimes commit crimes of violence out of a conviction that this is the only way they can right a wrong. Convictions that are based on faith in God are anchored in the truth and goodness of who God is and what God has done. Without such an anchor, convictions may be no more than "honor among thieves."

On the other hand, a profession of faith without conviction is empty and counts for nothing. In one of the letters of the New Testament, the apostle James writes to some would-be Christians: "You believe that there is one God. Good! Even the demons believe that—and shudder." Confession of faith that doesn't show itself by actions, the apostle adds, is meaningless and dead.

My father did not defend his refusal to thresh grain on Sunday by citing religious reasons. His words had no mention of church or worship: "I have never had to work on Sunday to get my work done, and I am not about to start now." Certainly this rule of life was rooted in his faith. But I would venture to say that the conviction behind that rule of life came not from reciting creeds or attending Sunday school as a young boy, but from the examples of his own parents and other Christians who lived out their faith in everyday life.

✴ CONVICTIONS ARE WHAT CHARACTER IS ABOUT

Convictions are what make us dependable people when the odds are against us and we're tempted to cut and run. It is not where we take a stand that makes conviction a value, but that we do take a stand. It is not the importance of the issue or the magnitude of the battle that determines the depth of a person's convictions. Heroism is not achieved by accomplishing a magnificent feat or losing one's life in a glorious battle. The true test of conviction is in the ordinary affairs of life.

We may not always find the most noble cause or the most prominent place to make our stand. In the midst of life's pressures to give way to seemingly insurmountable odds or to retreat until we find something worth fighting for, we may have to take a stand and defend something that seems silly to others and not of much significance to us.

I found such an example in the Bible.

In his account of the twilight of King David's life, the chronicler lists the names of thirty "mighty men," David's warriors who gained renown through heroic exploits. Some are simply names, while the deeds of three who were closest to David are noted as worthy of remembering. Shammah is listed as one of these three warriors. The Israelites under David's leadership were gathered in battle against the Philistines. "Where there was a plot of ground full of lentils; . . . the army fled from the Philistines. But he [Shammah] took his stand in the middle of the plot, defended it, and killed the Philistines; and the Lord brought about a great victory" (2 Sam. 23:11-12; see also 1 Chron. 11:12-13).

I will never forget the first time that I read this account. I was struck by the fact that the deed for which this warrior was remembered took place in the midst of a lentil field. We are told that he "took his stand in the middle of the plot, and defended it." To this man, the field represented not merely an insignificant piece of the land he was sworn to defend, but the entirety of it. To give up this small plot was to surrender his oath to the enemy.

Our characters are molded by the conviction with which we defend small things as if they were everything.

It is easy to give away our life in small pieces. A few hours on a Sunday morning, what is the importance of missing that? For my father, those hours may have represented the whole of his life. And he took his stand in the middle of that rather insignificant plot and defended it. We surrender our faith in small pieces when convictions are sacrificed to the expediency of the moment.

What can we teach our children and the next generation about character? The finest belief system held without convictions produces instability and shallowness of character. Belief cannot produce character, unless it is backed by convictions that have been put to the test. Without convictions we become "the hollow men" T. S. Eliot described in his poem by the same name:

> We are the hollow men
> We are the stuffed men
> Leaning together
> Headpiece filled with straw. Alas!
> Our dried voices, when
> We whisper together
> Are quiet and meaningless
> As wind in dry grass
> Or rats' feet over broken glass
> In our dry cellar
> Shape without form, shade without colour,

chapter six

Paralysed force, gesture without motion;
Those who have crossed
With direct eyes, to death's other Kingdom
Remember us—if at all—not as lost
Violent souls, but only
As the hollow men
The stuffed men.

(T. S. Eliot, *Collected Poems 1909-1962,*
New York: Harcourt Brace & Company, 1963, p. 56)

We are increasingly becoming a child-centered culture. Parents seem obsessed with involving their children in a year-round variety of extracurricular activities. Attending the events in which their children are involved is considered mandatory. Parents have become cheerleaders on the sidelines, with their children the star performers.

Which is better: to have adults participating in the play of children or children participating in the work of adults?

I played basketball, football, and softball in school. But I doubt if my parents ever saw me hit a home run or shoot a basket. When there was basketball practice after school, my father only asked if I would be home in time for chores.

I don't recall feeling neglected because my parents weren't spectators and supporters at these events. For the most part, this was not expected of parents, unless they were assigned to drive cars to transport the team to an out-of-town game.

But that was a different age and a different culture. Perhaps it isn't fair to make a comparison or to judge which parent-child relationship is better. Some aspects of both, no doubt, would be best.

One thing is true in either case: children are likely to develop their own convictions about life and values from observing the actions of their parents and other adults in their own world.

One can teach rules of fair play and sportsmanship in a game, but the convictions that determine where one takes a stand in life are not found in the rule book.

I lament the fact that so few of our children have opportunity to experience the adult arena in which the convictions of their parents are lived out. When family time together is spent mostly with parents as cheerleaders and spectators for their children's activities, and children are not invited into their parents' world, it is difficult to model convictions—especially the ones that are costly.

🏏 CONVICTION IS WHAT COMMITMENT IS ALL ABOUT

My father was always known as a man of his word. This I came to realize through insights from those who knew him well. And in the small rural community where he was born, lived his life, and died, there was hardly anyone who did not know him well. People could depend on him because he stood by his convictions—even in ways that were costly to him.

I think of my father when I read the words of Psalm 15 in the Bible. The psalmist is describing the person who has the character appropriate to stand in the temple of God. These are persons, the psalmist says, who walk blamelessly and do what is right. They do no evil to their friends, and they "stand by their oath even to their hurt."

An oath is a binding promise, a solemn commitment. Convictions are costly. The price we pay in keeping a commitment may far exceed the value we receive. Those who "stand by their oath even to their hurt" are people that you and I would trust.

Seldom did my parents discuss their problems in front of us children. On one occasion, however, they did. I still remember that conversation at the supper table because of its intensity.

Several years earlier, my father had rented farmland from my mother's father. The terms were cash rent, rather than a share of the crop. Three dollars an acre, as I recall. There was a hailstorm that year, and the crop was a total loss.

My mother was angry, and her anger was directed at her father. "I cannot understand why he is not willing to release us from paying the cash rent," she said. "Neighbors were good enough to bring over grain to replace what we lost, and here my own father still expects us to pay that money when we don't have it."

My father listened quietly. Then he said, "Alma, we made a deal, and we will keep it. Sooner or later we will find the money, and he will have his money, and that will be the end of it. So let it go."

I'm not sure that she did let it go. After all, it was her father, and she felt she had a right to expect from him as much as what came from the neighbors. But she knew well enough not to argue with my father about it any longer. For him, a deal was a deal, and he would keep his word to his own hurt.

All human relations are built on promises given and commitments made. To give birth to a child is to undertake an implicit commitment on the part of both parents to provide a nurturing, safe, and loving environment for the development of that new life. Children themselves enter into an implicit commitment to their parents and caretakers by receiving that love and care.

More explicit commitments are made in the form of vows and contracts such as those between marriage partners and employer and employee. There is an underlying assumption to life that commitments and promises are binding, that the commitments we make have the character of dependability about them.

Both the implicit and the explicit commitments we make in life are pieces of our character. If we give away one piece, we have damaged the whole. If we break one promise because keeping it is too costly, we tear away at our own character. And we damage the characters of those who know and trust us.

I don't believe my father ever gave me a moral lecture or taught me lessons about the Christian faith. Yet, in his own way, he had a greater influence on my life than any teacher or church ever had. He showed me what it meant to live according to convictions and, in so doing, he taught me what faith is really about.

Follow the curve and contour your life to the land

 or reasons that lie hidden within the secret heart of the farmer, planting a straight row of corn has always been a measure of pride. My father was no exception. As we would drive along the roads, he pointed out the fields of his neighbors, offering comments about how their crops looked.

"You see that, son?" he would say, stopping the car on the side of the road. "You see how those rows are crooked? I guess Carl must have dozed off when he was planting!"

My father's attitude was dead serious, as I was to find out when I first drove the two-row horse-drawn corn planter. After a few rounds, the tracks of the planter wheels were bending here and there as one looked down the field. "You've got to do better than that," my father said. He was not impressed by my argument that one could get more corn in a row that curved than one that went straight!

"When it comes time to cultivate, you will find patches of weeds where the rows are too wide," was his response. With that, he showed me how to keep the horses on a straight line by sighting down the field instead of following exactly the marker left by the previous trip. In that way, corrections could constantly be made, and the row kept straight.

Well, I learned how to plant in straight rows, to his satisfaction and my own pleasure. Up and down the hills, across the dips in the field, the rows went straight as an arrow. I liked to think that when cars drove down the road they were all admiring my expertise!

Near the end of my father's farming career, he began to talk a different game. It seems that he had become friendly with the county agricultural agent, whose job it was to advise farmers on better methods of crop rotation, seed selection, and cultivation of the soil.

"You see how the tops of the hills are covered with nothing but clay, and the topsoil has washed down into the ravine?" my father pointed out one day. "The rain runs straight down the hill and carries the soil with it. That's why nothing grows very well on the tops of the hills."

With that, he hired a surveyor to come out and set up stakes that curved around the hills at the same elevation. "It's called contour farming," my father explained. "When we plow and plant, we follow those stakes. The rows will serve as little dams to hold the water and keep the soil from washing." It was mostly an experiment on his part. I noticed that he tried it out on the north forty acres, where no one could see it from the road!

The method had its own logic, even though it violated the logic of many generations, where planting in straight rows was the measure of one's craft. It must have taken a good deal of inner struggle for my father to accept this new method. To abandon a custom that has been handed down from one generation to another is not easy. Some customs become virtually sacred, and to violate them seems like blasphemy that may bring down a curse upon the head of the offender. Farmers have enough bad luck anyway, and to risk divine disfavor is the last thing one needs!

On the other hand, my father had an innovative streak in him that never really had a chance to develop. On the occasion of his sister's ninetieth birthday celebration, she told me about a time when my father decided to run away from home when he was a teenager. It seems that one of his friends on another farm had told him about a different way of hitching horses, one that worked better than the old way. When he came from his friend's, he insisted on trying it out. His father would have none of those newfangled ways, as he put it. As a result, my father went into the house and announced that he was leaving home. His sister and his mother finally talked him out of it. Shortly after that, when my father was only eighteen years old, his father died. He became the head of the household, managing the farm for his mother and the brothers and sisters. My father's brief experiment with youthful radicalism was over, and he joined the ranks of the tried and true.

Now, toward the end of his career, he began to think outside the lines again. In his willingness to try out the new idea of contour farming, my father seemed to be giving me permission to try out new ideas and methods in my own life, rather than becoming rigid and conformed to the old.

In later years as I reflected on this, I thought about the difference between straight-row and contour farming as a kind of parable of life.

THE STRAIGHT-ROW APPROACH TO LIFE

In planting straight rows, we impose our own will on the soil. Where the land curves, we straighten it. When it undulates, we level it. We treat the soil as inert and lifeless, having no beauty until we impose our design on it, having no value until we plunder its riches for our crops. To our minds, beauty requires a sense of order—our sense of order—and this means correcting the promiscuous fluctuation and flow of nature by imposing on it our system of order.

Planting in straight rows up and down the hills is a way of

proving one's mastery over the land. There is a kind of stubbornness about it. The horses work harder to pull the plows uphill, and so the whip is brought out. Their natural instincts to take the easy way around are curbed. The mental image of a straight line is drawn like a ruler over the undulating land. The inert will of the land is made subservient to the will of the farmer. The passing observer no longer sees the natural lay of the land, but the rigid mind and control of the farmer. Straight rows become the measure of the man, demonstrating his triumph over the land. This is the sign of what we call an intelligent life-form!

A straight-row approach to life, like straight-row planting, tends to be rigid and intolerant. No deviation is permitted from the straight line toward the goal. When someone throws a curve into the plan, it is treated as a threat to be eliminated. This often means the end of a relationship or the loss of an associate. When people can become curves in our otherwise orderly life, they become dispensable. The insistence that one hew to the line allows no tolerance of personal idiosyncrasies or impulses. The introduction of change and novelty is upsetting and disorienting. When we view life from this perspective, we invest a good deal of energy and time in straightening and correcting.

This straight-row approach also tends to be perfectionistic and judgmental. Only what fits our predetermined standards is acceptable; everything else is an error. We often attach a moral value to keeping things in order. Anyone who does not maintain the same rigid discipline is viewed as unworthy or even immoral. The kindest thing to be said about those who do not follow the rules is that they are lazy or simply incompetent.

"I guess Carl must have dozed off when he was planting," my father said on that day when he was still practicing straight-row planting. He was being kind. On other occasions I knew my father to view Carl as lazy and shiftless. Beneath his attempt at humor was thinly veiled contempt. A common characteristic of the perfectionist is the use of derogatory and demeaning words in referring to "offenders."

The straight-row approach is often not so benign as to stop with contempt. When we place value judgments on another's work we also say something about that person's moral worth. Those who do not conform to our rules can be made to feel invisible, like a naughty child who becomes the "black sheep" of the family, or an oddball uncle whose name is never mentioned. When allowed to take its course, such moralism or perfectionism can lead to self-righteous attempts at eradicating those considered deviants.

It is dangerous to be a beautiful flower growing outside the lines in the field of the straight-row person! For everything not growing in the row is considered a weed. Such a mentality is described in the biblical accounts of Jesus' clashes with the authorities of his time. When Jesus refused to conform to the countless rules they had developed, they judged and condemned him: "This man is not from God because he does not observe the sabbath. . . . it is better to have one man die than to have the whole nation destroyed" (John 9:16; 11:50).

As I have suggested, the straight-row approach to life also can be stubborn and unyielding. When resistance is met, one gets out the whip and forces the beast up the hill.

I have one painful memory in this regard concerning my father. One of the six horses that we used for drawing farm implements was something of a rebel. For the most part, the animal was cooperative, but when pushed beyond its natural compliance, it would defy my father. On one occasion when the animal balked and refused to pull along with the others, my father became angry and, yes, stubborn. He got out the whip and began to beat the horse with it. The horse became enraged and struggled to get free. The battle continued while I watched in shock and disbelief. In the end, my father won. The horse stood dejected and shivering in confusion and pain. It was hardly a glorious victory.

When I protested, my father simply said, "Son, you can't let them get control. If I had let him get away with that, he would never be any good." My sympathies were with the horse. To this day, I find it hard to accept the idea of breaking the spirit of another creature in order to force it to comply.

Straight-row persons also use the whip a good deal on themselves. Self-punishment can become a goad to greater effort as well as a penalty for failure to measure up. Chronic anxiety is a by-product of such an approach to life. We anticipate disorder and deviation even before we experience them, and the adrenaline starts to flow. The whip is always in one hand, our muscles always tensed, our arm always raised. The emotional energy needed to sustain this state of readiness is enormous, and it diverts us from taking up more creative and fulfilling tasks and pleasures.

🌿 THE CONTOUR APPROACH TO LIFE

In contour farming, the natural lay of the land determines our use of it. The land is a partner in the process. We need its resources in order to produce our crops, and the land needs our cultivation and care in order to yield its harvest. Our relation to the land is one of sensitivity: we pay attention to its shape and form. The lay of the land shapes our hand and guides our cultivation of it.

When a field is contoured and the crop is growing, the natural form of the land is accentuated by the crops that cover it. Portions that are not cultivated are sown with grass and mown for hay. Instead of bearing an imposed, rigid design, the field takes on its own natural form as though proud of what it bears.

Contour farming has its own design and order. It is not chaotic and random, as though every impulse should be followed and every whim given the status of divine direction. There is discipline involved in contouring a field, but it is of a different kind than in straight-row planting. One approaches the task of laying out the contour lines by reading the lay of the land. For example, one works around the slope of hills, shaping the route so as to maintain a level line rather than a straight line. Where there is a natural flow of water, the soil is protected by sowing grass so that the sod forms a cover to prevent washing. Irregular areas that result where contour lines come up against rigid property lines are planted with trees or become an orchard, preserving the usefulness of the areas as part of the overall design.

Viewed from the air, a contoured farm is a mosaic of patterns accented by the cultivated crops and plantings, each portion fitting into the whole according to its own natural form.

A contoured field is a natural work of art as contrasted with the stiffness and monotony in straight-row fields, where every foot of the design is imposed without regard for its natural fit.

As in contour farming, the contoured approach to life involves working smarter rather than working harder. In this approach, the load is shared by the land. In other words, by keeping a level line around the slope rather than charging straight up the hill, the load becomes more manageable. No whip is needed to force greater effort or to punish for failure.

It takes more time to practice contour farming—careful planning and a thorough study of the land take time—but the results are worth it. Contoured rows provide a series of barriers to halt the washout effect of a sudden downpour. The hard work invested is saved from destruction and productivity is increased. Straight-row planting may be more time-and-effort efficient, but efficiency is too often the enemy of effectiveness.

The byword of modern technology is efficiency: new products promise to save us time, save us money, save us work.

Efficiency appeals to us in our crowded, rushed lives. We look for the fastest, easiest way—the shortest distance between two points—and so we mold our lives along straight lines, straight-row planting.

But people are made up of contours, not straight lines. The way to the heart of another person—or children, our spouse, our friend—is rarely a straight line.

When we take a contour approach to life, we enter our relationships and our tasks by first exploring the territory, "getting the lay of the land," to use the language of the farm. This means investing time and effort to examine the contours of another person's hopes, wishes, fears, insecurities. It means putting aside "efficiency" and the paradigm of straight-row thinking, with its rigidity, perfectionism, and stubbornness.

The contoured way of living will appear chaotic and inefficient when viewed through the old paradigm. In contour farming, there are always irregularities and odd patches that at first don't seem to fit. When we have lived with the obsession that everything must be in its place and have a place, it is difficult to accept the "odd patches" into the pattern of our lives.

I suspect that it would be difficult for a good flag maker to become a good quilt maker. The stars and stripes of the flag are carefully arranged in a set, rigid pattern. The quilt maker often creates as she sews, working with the pieces that are available, building a design that will incorporate the irregular patches.

My father planted corn in straight, rigid rows, like stripes on the flag. My mother was a good quilt maker. Both began to influence each other by the end, and they made a good team!

In retrospect, I see that my father was better at contour living than he was at contour farming. Although he planted in straight rows, his life was shaped more by events and experiences that came his way than by a pattern of his own imposing. When he attempted to leave the farm to help his brother operate an auto dealership and garage, the venture failed and he returned to the farm.

When the drought hit in the 1930s, he had just made a down payment on the only farm he ever tried to buy. Because of crop failures, he never was able to make another payment, and the title reverted to the bank.

When there was no market for our huge corn crop, he raised a herd of pigs and fed the corn to them.

When it came time to sell the pigs, the market was so bad that he lost money on them. After shipping a boxcar load of pigs to sell in Minneapolis, some two hundred miles away, he got a telegram back with a bill: the cost of shipping had exceeded the price paid for the pigs. My father wired back, tongue in cheek: "I don't have any money, but I'm sending more pigs!"

As he rode the up-and-down contours of his life, my father never lost his sense of humor or his sense of self-worth.

Following the curve of the land makes the load easier to bear.

Let the rhythm of life carry some of the risk

y father used to plant potatoes every spring. First we would cut them into pieces, making sure that each piece had an "eye" in it. From this eye, a sprout would form, and then the pieces were ready to be placed in the ground. One thing remained, however, before we could plant. To ensure a good harvest of potatoes, my father said, we must plant them when the moon is full. So we would wait until the propitious time and then place them in the ground.

Come fall, we always had sufficient potatoes, as I recall. In those days, I did not venture to submit my father's folk wisdom to a scientific test by deliberately planting some potatoes during another phase of the moon. I doubt that he ever did either. It was the only superstition that I recall my father including in his otherwise commonsense approach to the tilling of soil and the husbandry of livestock.

As I write this, I feel a sense of uneasiness in making such a clear distinction between superstition and common sense. My father would not have been happy to be called superstitious. For him, to work the soil was to participate in a cycle of sowing and reaping, suffering crop failures and rejoicing at bountiful harvests. His life as a farmer was lived in communion with the seasons of nature, with the rhythm of birth, life and death, and, yes, with the phases of the moon! This may be the most common of all senses.

🌟 MOON FABLES AND FOLLIES

There is something about the moon that holds a fascination for humans. The magic of its reflected glow has the power to draw the earthbound heart to its transcendent silvery beauty.

From ancient days the moon has had a powerful influence on humans—and not always a positive one. Romans called the moon *luna,* from which we have derived the word "lunacy," a state of mental disorder originally attributed to the phases of the moon. Even the ancient Israelites felt awe and apprehension about the moon. In the biblical book of Psalms, the poet alludes to that apprehension in his assurance of God's protection by day and night: "The sun shall not strike you by day, nor the moon by night" (Ps. 121:6). The term "moonstruck" once provided a ready explanation for irresponsible passion as well as irrational action. Even today we sometimes use the term. Who could deny the spell that moonlight can weave to incite passion and desire?

The origin of the folk wisdom that held potatoes should be planted when the moon was full is unknown to me. My father accepted that wisdom along with other bits of moon lore, such as a ring around the moon portending stormy weather. The latter may well have a more scientific basis according to those who study cloud particles, temperature, and such meteorological phenomena.

Fascinating as the moon is, my point is not to explore lunar power but to examine the human need for some cosmic assurance that can tame the terror of life's erratic and capricious nature. I have reason to believe that more people rely on a daily horoscope reading than on biblical texts. And even when they read the Bible, many people are searching its pages for some hidden clue or code to unlock the future, to reveal divine "tips" for how to live their lives.

In an Old Testament book that many attributed to King Solomon, supposedly the wisest person in ancient Israel, the writer admits he is blind with regard to humanity's helplessness in the face of inscrutable and capricious fate:

> Again I saw that under the sun the race is not to the swift, nor the battle to the strong, nor bread to the wise, nor riches to the intelligent, nor favor to the skillful; but time and chance happen to them all. For no one can anticipate the time of disaster. Like fish taken in a cruel net, and like birds caught in a snare, so mortals are snared at a time of calamity, when it suddenly falls upon them.
>
> (Eccles. 9:11-12)

The writer concludes that it is no use attempting to anticipate the hidden hand of destiny, so one might as well get on with life and make the most of every moment:

> Send out your bread upon
> the waters,
> for after many days you will
> get it back.
> Divide your means seven ways,
> or even eight,
> for you do not know what
> disaster may happen on
> earth.
> When clouds are full,
> they empty rain on the earth;
> whether a tree falls to the south
> or to the north,
> in the place where the tree
> falls, there it will lie.

Whoever observes the wind will
not sow;
and whoever regards the
clouds will not reap. . . .

In the morning sow your seed, and at evening do not let
your hands be idle; for you do not know which will pros-
per, this or that, or whether both alike will be good.

(Eccles. 11:1-6)

And now back to my father's annual nod to the "cosmic potato god." Was this some sort of attempt to magically influence
the hidden hand of fate? Was my father hoping to appease an
unknown master of destiny? Certainly not! The calamities that
can befall a potato crop are no greater than other misfortunes
to which farmers are subject. The fact is, potatoes are among
the vegetables least vulnerable to disaster, given sufficient water
and an occasional spraying for potato bugs. So why this yearly
ritual? I can explain it only as a relic of folklore and, more likely,
a small way of placing his life within the rhythm of nature.

🏹 WHAT YOU DON'T KNOW CAN HURT YOU!

There is something to be said for moving with the rhythm of
life, going with the flow of nature. "For everything there is a season, and time for every matter under heaven," says the writer of
Ecclesiastes. In the world of nature, both plants and animals
have their seasons of fertility, of mating, of shedding the old and
beginning anew.

The Bible describes how Jesus used examples from nature
when he counseled his followers against the kind of anxiety that
comes from attempting to control every aspect of life: "Look at
the birds of the air; they neither sow nor reap nor gather into
barns, and yet your heavenly Father feeds them. Are you not of
more value then they? . . . Consider the lilies of the field, how

they grow; they neither toil nor spin, yet I tell you, even Solomon in all his glory was not clothed like one of these" (Matt. 6:26-29).

The point of Jesus' illustration was to remind his followers that all living things have in common a loving Creator who can be trusted to care for them. What we do not have in common with birds and flowers is our destiny. The Bible tells us that human destiny is firmly in the hand of the Creator who loves and cares for us. And our destiny as God's children is to be God's partners and heirs of a joyful life that goes beyond the misfortunes of this world, even beyond the grave—a life with God that never ends.

From whence, then, comes anxiety? Why did our cows munch peacefully the last bit of hay and lie down with contentment to chew their cud, while my father spent a sleepless night wondering how he was going to buy food for them the next day?

Our anxiety is rooted in the knowledge of our own mortality: our bodies are subject to eventual decay and return to dust. This aspect of our earthly destiny stares us in the face every day. It is unavoidable. What we lose sight of in those anxious moments is the eternal destiny that is provided and promised by God, our Creator.

LETTING THE RHYTHM OF LIFE CARRY SOME OF THE RISK

In today's technological and often artificial world, we have lost more than our roots: we have lost touch with the rhythm of life. We can keep our houses and cars at an even temperature, no matter how hot or cold it is outside. We can buy fresh fruit in the winter and go ice skating in the summer. We can go to a zoo to see animals in their "natural habitat," wear synthetic fiber that feels like real wool, and furnish our homes with "authentic" replicas of traditional furniture.

chapter eight

Few of us worry about whether our potatoes will grow or whether the hail will destroy our harvest, but another risk attends our lives today that is just as real. The risk of which I speak is the personal investment of life with an uncertain return on the investment. How do we know that all of our efforts will result in a fulfilled life?

Planting potatoes during the full moon in hopes of a good harvest is a metaphor for the uncertain relation between what we do with our lives and what comes of them. This is the risk that factors we cannot control, events we cannot predict, and evil we cannot prevent will cause everything we do to fall to ruin.

My father lived in the face of these risks just as we all do, though his way of life was different and the way in which he coped may have been more quaint and provincial. But he found a rhythm in his life that helped carry the risks for him.

Let me see if I can relate this rhythm of life to our own time and place and explore several ways of capturing it.

First, life itself contains a rhythm when we see it as a whole, as a shared experience. Our existence is not an isolated series of individual episodes taking place as points in time. Rather, life involves us in a common pilgrimage. At any given time, we are part of a community where birth and death, joy and sorrow, pain and pleasure, as well as sowing and harvest are taking place. These communal experiences are the rhythms, the seasonal cycles, of life. For every milestone in our life—birth, love, marriage, failure, sadness, death—there is a pulse in the life of the human family. This collective rhythm is meant to help carry the risk of each person's existence.

My father was not just a farmer who raised crops; nor was he simply a husband, brother, father, or godparent. He was also part of all those who lived in his community. When there was a funeral, my father attended the services and often helped to carry the casket. When there was a wedding, my father joined in the celebration. When neighbors' children were born, my father rejoiced with the new parents. My father was part of—*one* with—the world in which he lived. He was part of the rhythm of life that surrounded him. And the strength that came from that shared rhythm bore him along and eased the risks of his life. In no way could a crop failure or business loss rob him of his value and place in the community.

Second, there is a rhythm in the blessing and celebration of each individual life. The blessing of a newborn baby, for instance, is not only a religious ritual, but it is the human family's way of bearing the risk of that child's life. The blessing says that this child belongs, this child counts, this child's life is woven into the "quilt" of the community in such a way that there will always be a place for it, no matter how "irregular" its shape!

The blessing of a family upon its children reminds them and assures the community that God's love is reflected down upon that small life. What cannot be controlled, what cannot be predicted, and what cannot be prevented is brought under the blessing of God. The risk is shared.

The reality of this rhythm of divine love in the community of early Christians is reflected in the apostle Paul's New Testament letter to the church at Rome:

> If God is for us, who is against us? . . . For I am convinced that neither death, nor life, nor angels, nor rulers, nor things present, nor things to come, nor powers, nor height, nor depth, nor anything else in all creation will be able to separate us from the love of God in Christ Jesus our Lord.

> (Rom. 8:31, 38-39)

This is what it means for one's life to be blessed by birth into the family of God, the human community in which the Spirit of God dwells.

Third, there is a rhythm that comes from the sabbath rest

which was commanded by God at the beginning of time. The Genesis account of creation concludes with God's institution of this day of rest: "Thus the heavens and the earth were finished, and all their multitude. And on the seventh day God finished the work that he had done, and he rested on the seventh day from all the work that he had done. So God blessed the seventh day and hallowed it, because on it God rested from all the work that he had done in creation" (Gen. 2:1-3).

The repeated refrain of God resting "from all the work that he had done" reminds us that our work also is to be followed by rest. The sabbath—the day of rest—is blessed and hallowed because this is the time for us to put aside work and turn with refreshed, renewed attention to something else. On the sabbath, God's people no longer focus on their work, but on the work of their loving God.

There is work, there is an end to work, there is rest. A weekly rhythm.

Without the sabbath as a blessed interlude, human life would be unbearable. Even the most joyful work would become a relentless routine of toil and drudgery.

I picture the ancient Israelites, on the eve of the sabbath, turning their backs to the toil and labor of six days and saying to the earth: "You have no power over us! For twenty-four hours we are under the gracious care and provision of our creator God." Every six days, this rhythm of a sabbath rest became a source of renewal and re-creation. Each new week became a new beginning.

At the supper table after one particularly long and grueling day, in which my father and I had worked at a task in which virtually nothing went right, he said, "Well, no matter how long and hard the day, at the end it's just one day's work. Tomorrow is another day." It was his way of saying, "Today's work is finished. Tomorrow we can start anew."

It is often difficult for people today to have a sense that anything is finished. Their work seems to be never ending. They can never leave it behind. This means that there is no rhythm of renewal, no sabbath rest, built into their lives.

It is unfortunate that the concept of the sabbath has become primarily a religious ritual to be defined and enforced by the church. Perhaps it is time to recover an understanding of the sabbath as a practice of renewal as well as a day to go to church.

We cannot begin anew until something is finished. My father had a knack for knowing when to quit for the day. He was in no hurry to plant the potatoes; he could wait for the full moon. For everything there was a time and season.

Being who you are is all you need to be

hortly after my eighteenth birthday, I enlisted in the Army Air Force. I had mixed motives. The United States was almost two years into the Second World War, and I preferred to choose my own destiny rather then wait to be drafted into the infantry. I suspect that my decision was also prompted by an element of patriotism mixed with romanticism. I often wonder how my parents felt when I came home with this announcement. I have no memory of consulting with them on the decision, nor of their resistance to the idea. Preoccupation with one's future has a way of blinding one to others' reactions and feelings.

Within a couple of months, my father drove me to the train station in the nearby town. He sat quietly while I got out of the car. Not looking directly at me, he shook my hand, and with a quaver in his voice said, "Remember who you are, Ray, and you will be all right." Out of respect for his sense of decorum, I pretended not to notice the single tear that crept down my father's cheek, and I shed none of my own. Only now, as I write this, can I weep.

A single tear. But all the more precious because of it! I know people who weep at the slightest occasion. I know men who shed tears without embarrassment. But I remember only that single tear on my father's face in all of the years of knowing him. It is not as though he never had other occasions to grieve or feel strong emotion. But I remember only one tear.

One tear is sufficient to bear proof of simultaneous unspoken love and heartrending pain. The Bible describes only one occasion when Jesus wept, and that was at the tomb of his friend Lazarus. It may have been only a single tear. But it had divine significance.

Yet it was not my father's tear that I carried with me, but the words that he spoke. "Remember who you are, Ray, and you will be all right."

This was not the first time he had used that expression. The other occasion was some years earlier, when my younger sister was about to leave for an out-of-town trip with a group from her class. This was the first time she had ever been away from home. We were sitting around the supper table when she expressed concern about whether she would know what to do and how to do it. I was vaguely aware that she and my mother were talking about the trip. My mother was attempting to reassure her.

Suddenly I heard my father say, "Just remember that you are Myla, that's all you need to be. You will be all right." He must have been right, for, as I recall, she had a good time. And, from what I know of my sister, I suspect that she has followed that bit of advice for all these years.

I wonder how many fathers would have felt compelled to give their sons a long lecture as they went off to military service, warning them about the temptations and dangers, offering advice, and exhorting them to good behavior. In retrospect, I find my father's restraint amazing and, at the same time, quite understandable. He was a man who lived by his own convictions and believed that his children could do the same.

What is even more amazing is that I understood what he

meant and felt reassured by his words. I knew that whatever obstacles and uncertainties I would face, I would be able to maintain my own identity and integrity.

✈ BECOMING WHO WE ARE

The simple affirmation, "Remember who you are," is not so simple, as it turns out. Being "who we are" involves a complex and often difficult process of discovering and affirming our own identity. Young people who don't have a strong sense of identity often succumb to peer pressure, in order to be whom others want them to be. The need to belong and to be affirmed is so strong that we can be drawn to others like a magnet if we do not have our own "magnetic field," so to speak.

Several themes have emerged in this book that relate to the issue of knowing who we are. One is the importance of having solid convictions and standing up for them, even in matters that might appear trivial or insignificant to others. Convictions, as I pointed out, are not the same as a confession of faith that can easily be set aside when it becomes costly. Convictions are gained by standing alongside people who have them and live by them. Children do not acquire convictions from other children, but from adults who are closest to them.

I have expressed my belief that it is more important for children to be drawn into the lives of their parents than for the parents to be cheerleaders for their children's activities. As valuable as it is for parents to participate in their children's lives, it is more essential that children participate—become partners—in the adult tasks and responsibilities of their parents' world.

When my father sent me back out to mow the field a second time, he gave me an adult responsibility: to finish well the work that I had started. This experience did more to help me develop a sense of identity than hearing him cheer as I hit a home run in a softball game or shot the winning basket in a basketball game.

When my father expressed confidence in me by suggesting that I could ride the horse I feared, another piece was added to "who I was."

The primary factors that contribute to a child's self-identity are not peer relationships, but relationships with significant adults. When they are wholesome and nurturing, such child-adult relationships can enable us to acquire convictions, a sense of responsibility for our own task in life, and an appreciation for our individual uniqueness and value.

There are some parents, I fear, who exploit their children by giving them adult duties without supplying the confidence and the model that can empower such tasks. This kind of exploitation rarely provides growth, and it can rob the children of their childhood.

Making a child act like an adult is quite different from empowering a child to grow into a mature and adult self.

My father did not treat me like an adult or make me act like an adult. While he did not enter into the games and play of my childhood, he allowed time for them. At the same time, he exposed me to his own struggles and convictions in such a way that I could stand with him and alongside him. As appropriate, he gave the reins over to me, and allowed me to grow into his tasks and duties. It wasn't that I was expected to perform these tasks "like a man," but rather that I was given the chance to take on the tasks of a man, to begin claiming them for myself.

This is it! This is the difference. I was gradually allowed to have ownership of things that counted, things that could offer more fulfillment than the marbles I won through sharpshooting expertise. Empowerment does not come through words of praise but through ownership of tasks and responsibility.

One of the horses that we used on the farm was not like the other workhorses. This one was not built for heavy work, though he was put into the harness for lightweight tasks. A beautiful *chapter nine*

shade of burnished black, the horse had a sheen in his coat and sparkle in his eyes. The animal had a different spirit from the others. There was something free and adventurous about him. At the slightest urging he would break into a gallop, as though pleased to be given free rein.

In my early teens, this horse became "my" riding horse. On Sundays, I would spend hours exploring the nearby countryside with him. During the summer, it was my task to herd the cows in unfenced areas when the pastures became dry and parched. This horse was my companion in the task.

That summer a strange disease began to afflict horses in the area. It was called "sleeping sickness" because when it struck, the horse quickly became paralyzed and could not walk. It was incurable and dreaded.

One day my father walked into the house and said in an even tone, "One of the horses is down. I think it is the sleeping sickness." "Which one?" I asked, with a sense of apprehension. "Not Blackie!"

"Yes," he replied. "I'm sorry. He is out in the pasture and can't get up. We will have to put him down. It's the only way to end his misery." He reached up and took down the 12-gauge shotgun we used for hunting. Then, looking closely at me, he said, "Do you want to do it? It's your horse."

I was stunned. Is it possible that my father could ask me such a question? How could he think that I would be able to kill Blackie?

The key, of course, was his statement "It's your horse." I had been permitted an unofficial ownership of Blackie as part of my responsibilities with him. When an animal has to be put down, the custom was for the owner to do it. This was part of the responsibility of ownership. But it was also more than that. The killing of an animal as an act of mercy is part of the bond between that animal and its owner. And when an animal has become your friend, friendship demands that you perform this last rite with dignity and kindness.

My father would have done it, of course. Blackie was officially his horse, and he accepted responsibility for what he owned. But he clearly understood that my "ownership" took precedence over his because my relationship with the animal was deeper and closer.

It was not out of consideration for Blackie that he invited me to perform the dreaded act. It was out of consideration for me. Not to have offered me the job would have been to take the responsibility away from me. It would have left me as a child whose plaything was gone, but who had no share in the grief and pain—and responsibility—of ending Blackie's misery. Nor would I have had a tangible way of dealing with my own loss. The animal would have simply "disappeared," and the hole that was left would be deeper and darker than any grave.

I did it. I was no stranger to the gun, having used it often for hunting pheasants and rabbits. I knew exactly what to do, for I had watched at other times when animals were disposed of. I went out alone. This was my task, as my father wisely understood. Once the deed was done, we buried Blackie in a shallow grave dug with another team of horses and an earth scraper.

We do not develop self-identities only through pleasant experiences and praise and good advice. We become full, self-assured persons by taking death as well as birth in stride, for that is to know the full measure of life. We become who we are by knowing clearly what is ours and taking responsibility to care for it to the very end.

✦ BEING WHO WE ARE

I count it of great significance that my father was able to speak the words "Remember who you are, Ray, and you will be all right." My father was a man of very few words. So much that passed between us was unspoken. The reins were placed in my hands without a lecture on plowing. He sent me back to finish my sloppy job of mowing without recrimination or scolding. Nor did he often reward me with words of praise for work well done—as if my own satisfaction in the job had no value unless it was honored by words.

But there are times when words of affirmation are important and even necessary. The unspoken must be said. The blessing must be given before it can be received. My leaving home for military service was one of those times. For all my father knew, these may well have been the last words that he would ever say to me. In saying them, he put the reins of my own life in my hands for good.

"*. . . my own life in my hands for good.*" On that leave-taking, my father not only handed me the reins of my life once and for all, he also handed me the responsibility of directing my life for good rather than for evil.

My father had lived his own life "for good." This is the goodness of doing something right the first time, the goodness of living by convictions even when they are costly, the goodness of taking responsibility for what is yours, the goodness of drawing his son into his own life and thereby preparing that son to enter adulthood.

From this point on—"for good"—it was my job to live as the man he had helped me become, to draw on "who I was" as I stepped out into the adult world. My father's parting words radiated confidence in me: "Remember who you are, Ray, and you will be all right."

What, then, does it mean to "Remember who you are"?

First, to remember who we are is to keep faith with what we have been taught, to confirm that teaching in our lives. When I was a young teenager, I successfully mastered several years of courses in Lutheran faith and doctrine. After the lessons were over, I publicly confessed my faith and was "confirmed" as a Christian in the same Lutheran church where my father was confirmed years before—although my confession was recited in English and his in Norwegian!

I had another kind of "confirmation service" with my father at the train station when I left for the service. (The lessons were over all too soon, my mother and father probably thought.) My father's words of confirmation—"Remember who you are, Ray, and you will be all right"—were an affirmation of everything I had learned, everything he hoped he had taught me. True, I was still immature and naive, but my father's work was done. I was off to a good start.

The determination to keep faith with who I was—even at this early stage of my life—became an automatic warning system when confronted with fear and temptation. My father's confirmation of the goodness within me became the inner resource of courage and conviction to deal with that which was not good in me or for me.

Second, to remember who we are is to honor those who have invested in our growth and sown the seeds for our future. When we honor our parents through acts of love and respect, when we honor their memory through reflection on their lives, we are also remembering who we are. Even as I write this book, I have come to realize that it is as much a way of remembering who I am as it is a tribute to my father.

The obligation to honor our parents is so important that it was made into one of the Ten Commandments: "Honor your father and your mother, so that your days may be long in the land that the Lord your God is giving you" (Exod. 20:12). And this is the only commandment to which a promise is attached!

Third, to remember who we are is to continually invest in our own becoming. Up to a point, the job of "growing up" is handled by our parents. But after their job is completed, a lot of growing and becoming still remains to be done. Now, the task is ours.

"You will be all right." Those were my father's words of blessing at my departure from home. I believe he was right, and I will continue to live with that promise. He put the reins in my hands as he bade me farewell. What more can a father do?

chapter ten

Moving out from another's shadow into your own sun

 had not read Thomas Wolfe's novel *You Can't Go Home Again* at the time that I returned from military service. Only years later did the truth of this book speak to the reality that I experienced in 1945 following the end of the Second World War.

The time I spent in the Army Air Force intensified the longing I had for the soil and deepened the conviction that I wanted to follow in my father's footsteps on the farm. My father had finally purchased a tractor, a small John Deere with steel wheels. (The effects of the war and the rationing of rubber tires were the explanation for the steel wheels.)

The tractor was a grudging submission to progress on my father's part, as I was to discover. He kept his stable of horses and used the tractor only for heavy work in the field. I, however, reveled in this transition into the twentieth century and used the tractor in preference to horses at every opportunity.

My father nursed a stubborn doubt over the practicality and necessity of a machine that thrived on costly gasoline while horses could live on grass, hay, and a helping of home-grown oats. In the spring, this doubt turned into thinly concealed delight when I mired the tractor up to its axle in the wet soil, and he brought out four horses to help pull it out.

"I never had a horse that couldn't get itself out of a mud

hole," he said as he drove away, leaving me to continue to work with the tractor.

Never mind. I was soundly converted to this product of the industrial revolution, and his scorn had little effect on my enthusiasm.

I was back home on the farm I loved. I had returned from the war with sound body and mind. And we were moving into the twentieth century. I was certain that the best was yet to come. But it was not to be.

My expectation, heightened by homesickness during the years of military service, was that I would come back to work with my father and everything would be the same. I did not mind standing in his shadow, for it was as long as the land itself, and as broad as the horizon of my dreams.

As we planted the crops that next spring, I envisioned a portion of the farm where I might sow my own seed and harvest my own crop. I offered a deal to my father. I would put in his crop, using his machinery, in exchange for a field of my own where I might begin to farm for myself.

His response was direct and devastating. "There is not room enough on this farm for both of us to make a living," he said. "I do not own the land, and have no income except for what I gain from this farm after giving a third of the crop to the owner. You will simply have to make it on your own."

To say that I was totally unprepared for this would be an understatement. My first response was disbelief and anger. But there was no room for argument. It was not a matter of changing his mind, as though he had made an arbitrary decision that could be shifted by persuasion. His logic was unassailable. He was stating a fact, not an opinion.

In something of a huff, I finally said, "If that's how it is going to be, I have college benefits coming to me as a veteran. I will enroll in agricultural college next fall." And so it was.

Some time later, my mother confided that this is exactly what my father hoped I would do. He wanted me to have opportunities he never had, and college was one of them.

My mother's words were confirmed after I had made the final arrangements to go. "You can always farm," he told me, "but you may not always have the opportunity to get more education."

I do not want to be misunderstood about this matter. My father's refusal to allow me to share the farm was not a tactic designed to force me off to college. At no time during our discussions about the farm did he suggest that my attending college would be his preference or to my advantage. His decision about the farm was based on fact. There was simply not room enough for both of us. At the same time, he apparently felt that I was quite capable of taking my own life in hand.

But was he not under some obligation to make room for me on the farm? What's a father for if not to help his son gain a foothold on the slippery slope of life? Was he not responsible in some way for assisting me to launch my career?

My father did not think so. When I assumed responsibility for my life, his obligation was over. Well, not absolutely. There would always be a place at the supper table and clean sheets on a bed, if worse came to worst. He would certainly agree with Robert Frost's poetic description: "Home is a place where, when you have to go there, they have to take you in."

My father was not disowning me, simply discharging his obligation to me. He knew that his duty to shield me from the sun and provide a space within his shadow was over. It was time for me to move out of his shadow into my own sun.

🖋 KNOWING WHEN AN OBLIGATION IS OVER

A sense of obligation can be both creative and crippling. And wise is the caregiver or parent who knows the difference.

One of the marks of maturity is a willingness to assume obligations. Sometimes these are thrust upon us, while at other times we can choose whether to accept them or not. When he was eighteen, my father had little choice but to assume the obligation of running the family farm when his own father died. In the trauma created by this sudden death and the family's loss of a husband and father, he stepped in to provide a home for his mother and five siblings.

My father's obligation toward his mother lasted for the duration of her life. She died in our home. One of my earliest memories is how, at the age of five or six, I stared with childlike wonder at her body lying in the casket in our home. As soon as his brothers and sisters were old enough to take responsibility for their own lives, my father's obligation as their caretaker ended and he became simply their brother.

When one person's obligation for another produces the positive values of growth and love, it is creative and full of promise. Behind the obligation is commitment to support and sustain the other's life for good in the face of all adversity and change. In my role as a minister, I include such obligations in the vows that I ask couples to recite at their wedding. The obligations in the wedding vows are based on trust in God and in one another, and they involve a lifelong commitment to mutual nurture and growth:

> From this day forward,
> I pledge my love and faithfulness to you,
> I promise to honor and respect you
> as a precious gift of God;
> I will encourage, support, and care for you,
> as we learn and grow together;
> I promise to be your friend and partner
> in spite of all changes and adversity,
> in sickness and health,
> in happiness as well as in hardship;

with God's help, I will uphold this covenant
as long as I shall live.

There is a darker and more destructive side to obligations, however, that can creep in on the unsuspecting. Obligations can become crippling when they become controlling and coercive.

Being under obligation to someone who uses that relationship to control and compel is demeaning and destructive to self-worth and growth. Power over others can become addictive. One way to turn a healthy obligation into a destructive power play is to continue the relationship beyond its purpose, using it to keep the obliged person weak and dependent upon the caregiver.

The parent-child relationship is vulnerable to the misuse of obligation, and marriage relationships also can shift from nurturing and healthy mutual obligation to destructive and crippling power plays in which one person's weakness is used to sustain the other's strength.

Children are naturally and rightly dependent upon parents for physical, emotional, and spiritual growth into mature persons. The power differential is obvious, though it need not be crippling if parents see their responsibility as developing their child's own sense of obligation. One of the primary tasks of parenting is to empower children to assume obligations. Parents are *obliged* to do this. This kind of obligation has the purpose of transferring power, so to speak. When the obligation has fulfilled its purpose—children are ready to take on their own obligations—so does the power that goes with it.

One example of this kind of obligation can be found in the biblical example of Jesus and his twelve closest followers. "You did not choose me," Jesus told them, "but I chose you. And I appointed you to go and bear fruit" (John 15:16). Having chosen twelve followers, Jesus had an obligation toward them. His strength was committed to their weakness, his clear vision to their uncertainty and confusion. At the end of three years of constant association and guidance, Jesus said to them, "I do not call you servants any longer, because the servant does not know what the master is doing; but I have called you friends, because I have made known to you everything that I have heard from my father" (John 15:15).

In a sense, Jesus was saying that his obligation to his followers was now over. They were now empowered to live and act without constant dependence on his physical presence and guidance. In a prayer to his Father, Jesus speaks of the obligation he has passed on to his followers: "As you have sent me into the world, so have I sent them into the world" (John 17:17).

Such an obligation is based on love: it is creative, nurturing, and empowering, and it knows when to "let go" and trust the other to take up the burden of obligation.

✳ YOU CANNOT CAST A SHADOW UNLESS YOU ARE STANDING IN THE SUN

Wisely, my father realized that his shadow was no longer necessary to shield me from the harsh and sometimes unfriendly rays of the sun. It was time for me to cast my own shadow. But one cannot cast a shadow without standing in the sun.

Leaving home can mean moving out of the shadow of another into our own sun. I thought I had moved out of my parents' shadow when I entered military service. From their perspective, I was no longer in their shadow. As it turned out, however, I took hold of their shadow and pulled it with me—fearing, I suppose, that if I let it go, it would roll back into itself like a blind that is released, leaving me exposed and naked.

This is not an uncommon experience.

We are told that more and more adult children are moving back into parental homes, primarily for economic reasons. But I wonder . . . Certainly the economic pressure of maintaining a home is costly and often prohibitive. But I suspect that in many cases there are other reasons for this return to the nest.

There is a pervasive sense of insecurity in our culture these days. Young people who are insecure about their new independence may be tempted to tuck the shadow of their parents under their belts and carry it with them, rather than trusting themselves to cast their own shadows. And when you never let go of your parents' shadow, you have never really left home—no matter how far away you move.

Parents are equally insecure about obligations to their children. Bowing to the accusation that today's parents fail to provide adequate emotional support during their children's early lives, they can easily succumb to feeling that they have an unfulfilled obligation that an extra bedroom, a place at the dinner table, and some financial assistance will satisfy.

And so the parents' shadow continues to loom over the child.

Moving out of the shadow into one's own place in the sun is not like a leap of faith or a kick in the pants. It may require a nudge and a bit of faith, but such a move is more the culmination of a process, like giving birth to a baby that has been growing and developing for a long time. The birth may be normal, natural, and nearly on time. Or, it may be premature, dangerously delayed, or delivered through cesarean section. In any event, viability is the criterion—the baby's ability to survive independent of the womb and the umbilical cord.

In the story of Peter Pan, we find the quintessential champion of children who refuse to grow up. Peter is inordinately proud of his shadow and, when it comes undone, he searches for Wendy to sew it back onto his foot. Children who refuse to grow up are likewise desperate to hold on to shadows, but these are not ones they cast themselves.

If moving out of the shadow of another into our own sun is

to be a natural and healthy process, several things must lead up to the event.

First, moving into our own sun requires confidence that we can cast our own shadow. The problem with standing in someone else's shadow is that one cannot see one's own. By the time my father informed me that there was no longer room for both of us on the same farm, he had made sure that I had already seen a shadow of my own. And if one has a shadow, then one is already standing in the sun.

Putting the reins of the horses in my hand and sending me out to plow the field alone led to some confusion, but the confusion and the solution were of my making. In giving me responsibility to dispose of the incurably ill horse, my father sent me out alone into the sun. After I had walked alone down the train platform to leave for the army, the last vision my father had of me was my shadow as I waited for the train door to open. When he drove home on that day, he knew that his obligation was over. My returning home could not renew his obligation. He had the sense to see that and bear the reproach of my disappointment and anger toward him.

I no longer needed the shadow of my father. He knew that before I did: he had led me into the sun. And when I looked for it, I was able to see my shadow. It was the confidence that I had in my own shadow that enabled me to walk out of his and take my place in the sun.

Less than four years after I left home, I was living on my own rented farm. When he and my mother came to visit, I was milking the three cows that I had managed to buy on borrowed money. As he watched me, my father suddenly said, "Well, son, it seems that you are just where you wanted to be." I believe that I said "yes," but I did not think to add "thanks to you." It's a bit late, but I am saying it now. This too is an obligation fulfilled.

Second, moving into our own sun means staying the course,

even when our sun disappears behind clouds. I sometimes have the romantic and sentimental notion that the sun is always shining at my childhood home, and that when storm clouds come into my sky, I can go back there and find it again.

That, of course, is an illusion. Our minds create such illusions to comfort our hearts when we think we can't endure the pain of our sunless days. Some people give in to that temptation and follow the illusion in hopes that they will find eternal sunshine and happiness by returning to their roots. As valuable as roots are, they are meant to stay underground in the soil from which we have come. Roots provide security, nourishment, and strength. They anchor us firmly and connect us to our past. But our hope must be in the flower that blooms in the sun—even though that flower may be blown about by winds and stormy skies.

When the sun goes behind clouds and the shadow that once marked our place vanishes, there is often a moment of panic that makes us reach out to those who once were obliged to provide our support. When we find them "settled in" and no longer able to support us, we feel abandoned and lost. Those who once were there to point the way have dropped behind and departed from our lives.

This is where our roots are important—the anchors that were built into our lives long ago. Through the example of his conviction and faith, my father was able to lead me to the beginnings of my own spiritual strength. In learning to be the son of my father, I learned to have faith in and live by the Son who called God his Father. This faith has carried me through many cloudy days and times of darkness.

Biblical accounts indicate that Jesus knew his followers would have times of darkness and despair. The Gospel of John describes how Jesus prepared them for such times: "Very truly," he told them, ". . . you will have pain, but your pain will turn into joy. When a woman is in labor, she has pain, because her hour has come. But when her child is born, she no longer remembers the anguish because of the joy of having brought a human being into the world. So you have pain now; but I will see you again, and your hearts will rejoice, and no one will take your joy from you" (John 16:20-22).

In the comfort of his promise "I will see you again," Jesus became a light that would see his followers through the cloudiest days. The Son of God becomes the Sun—a beacon of hope that continues to shine when all around goes dark.

chapter eleven

Learning to live means learning to die

he call came on an autumn day the year after I had completed college and moved to my first rented farm. My father, who had suffered for several years from cancer of the throat, had lapsed into a coma and was dying. Driving to the town where he and my mother lived, I reflected upon his life. He was sixty-four years old; I was twenty-four. At the time, I thought that sixty-four was pretty old. One's perspective does change, however, as the years go by. I have lived longer than he did by several years, and now realize what a youthful age that was!

Only a few months earlier, my father had visited our farm and, while watching me milk my three cows, had remarked that it seemed I'd finally found what I wanted in life. I gathered that it was also what he wanted for me. I did not know that these words would be his final blessing on my life.

At that time, he could talk only by holding one finger over the metal tube that had been inserted into his throat to force air through the damaged vocal cords. Poor health had caused him to give up farming several years earlier. It was the long habit of daily smoking that led to the cancer and his premature death. I say "premature death," but my father never expressed bitterness about dying at a relatively young age. He voiced no regret, did not blame himself, and did not protest against the unfairness of it all. He seemed to take it in stride without complaining. It was only as I drove the short distance to the home where he lay dying that I realized how calmly he had approached his death.

He was unable to speak, but he indicated that he could hear and understand what we were saying. He moved his eyes and made small gestures with his hands, as if to punctuate sentences that were in his mind. Within a few hours, even those responses ceased and he lay motionless except for occasionally raising his hand to rub his lower lip, a familiar gesture so common to him that it required no conscious thought. For nearly two days we watched as he grew weaker and weaker. The doctor, who had made a brief visit, told us that the end was near.

It was on a Sunday. The Lutheran minister arrived following the morning service and walked straight to my father's bedside. After a brief greeting to the family, he began to recite the Twenty-third Psalm: "The Lord is my shepherd, I shall not want. He makes me lie down in green pastures. He leads me beside still waters; he restores my soul." My father, who had not moved a muscle for several hours, suddenly raised his hands and folded them across his chest. Those words, which he had first heard so many years ago, brought a response, which assured us that God was already beginning to lead him beside still waters and restore his soul.

His heart stubbornly measured out his last hours like a bell, rhythmically tolling the seconds as they slipped away. With my hand on his chest, I felt the last shuddering beat, and then the stillness. His family acknowledged his death by each grieving in his or her own way. His sister took his teeth from the glass by his bed and placed them in his mouth. Placing a towel under his chin, she tied it over his head, restoring his face to quiet repose. Lowering his eyelids, she placed a coin on each. As I watched silently, I realized that she was performing a ritual that she had been taught and was training us to do as much for her. When the doctor arrived, he confirmed my father's death by filling out a formal certificate. Our family had already confirmed the death by our simple rituals of love.

✈ JOINED BY THE HEARTBEAT OF BIRTH AND DEATH

Holding my father's hands as his life slipped away, I realized that these were the hands that had held my newborn life and felt the pulse of my heart at birth. There is a time when hearts begin to beat, and there is a time when they stop. So begins and ends our allotted time on earth.

The mystery of death is intimately connected to the miracle of birth. Each is a gift. Each is part of the same continuum. One cannot embrace one without taking hold of the other.

My father had learned this lesson long ago. Death was never a stranger to his life: his entrance into adulthood began with the death of his father. Death introduced him to obligations— his duty to care for his mother and siblings, his responsibility to manage the family farm—that lasted a lifetime. His years were marked with other deaths as well: the death of his mother, the failure of crops and businesses, the death of livestock and horses.

But for every death there was also a birth. My father witnessed birth each year as the seeds he had sown burst into green and growing life. He rejoiced at the new life that came with the birth of his children. He saw his efforts as a father give birth to confident and responsible adults.

My father embraced it all—birth, death, and everything that came between. And he died as he had lived, with quiet faith in a loving God who had promised to lead him "beside still waters" and restore his soul.

It will not be given to many of us to feel the last heartbeat of one we love; nor is it likely that many of us will have our children near enough to feel our final heartbeats. In our contemporary culture, dying is no longer a ritual of life to be shared with family. It is usually an isolated experience confined to hospitals or nursing homes. And it is no longer viewed as a natural part of life, but as a failure of technology and medical science. The only death that most of us will directly experience is our own. But this should not catch us by surprise.

🌾 LIVING SO THAT DEATH IS NOT A SURPRISE

We should not be surprised by death, even if it comes when we don't expect it. As tragic as it may seem—and all deaths are a grievous loss—death is woven into the very fabric of life.

The farm on which we lived from the time I was five years old until my last year in high school adjoined the community cemetery just a mile or so out of town. Although it was separated by a fence from the pasture where our cows and horses grazed, the cemetery seemed almost like it belonged to us. On many an occasion I slipped through the fence to wander among the graves and play in the well house which supplied water for the flowers and grass.

Frequently on a Sunday afternoon, my father would announce, "We're going to the cemetery to tend the graves. Who's going along?" I almost always went. I enjoyed the stories my parents told as they went from grave site to grave site. "Here's where the Torstensons are buried. Wasn't she a Carlson girl who came over with her parents from the old country? Didn't they homestead the quarter section next to the old Anderson farm where I was born?" My father would ask the questions as though they had only just occurred to him and he actually expected someone to answer them. But they were not really questions. My father was reciting the history of our community.

On and on the questions went, calling the roll of our neighbors and ancestors and adding bits of information that brought them to life, if only for those fleeting moments.

I often wondered what my father thought when he passed a small grave marker and commented, "Yes, and here is the two-year-old Peterson boy. He was kicked in the head by a cow and died that very night." Did he question the fairness of that death? Had he ever questioned God about that?

What did he think about when he pulled weeds from the plot where he himself would someday be buried? Did he have anxiety? Did he fear that death would destroy all of the meaning of his life? Or did he have in his heart a conviction and hope that lay beyond the grave?

I don't know. He never said. Death and God were the two subjects never openly questioned. Both were assumed to be beyond doubt and, therefore, beyond question.

I think we were lucky to live so near that cemetery. Our frequent walks through the grave sites and our conversations about the people buried there made them seem like old friends. The dead became a part of our lives; death seemed almost comfortable to us.

At the same time, there was no preoccupation with death in our home. Because we lived with it each day, there seemed to be no need to live in fear of it. Grieving losses—stillborn cattle, hail-stricken crops, fatal injuries—were as much a part of life as celebrating birthdays and giving thanks for a bounteous harvest.

The Old Testament book of Job describes how the title character lost everything he possessed, including his family. His reaction was one of grief, but not of surprise; and throughout his suffering, he never lost faith in God. To his wife's angry demand that he "curse God and die," Job responded, "Shall we receive good at the hand of God, and not receive the bad?" (Job 2:10). Despite the misfortunes of life, Job maintained his integrity and faith. He expected God always to be there for him, especially during his time of suffering.

chapter eleven

Is genuine happiness possible amidst the certainty that life holds suffering, loss, and death? The film *Shadowlands*, based on the life of writer and theologian C. S. Lewis, explores this question. When Joy, the woman he marries late in life, is found to have incurable cancer, Lewis determines that they will make the most of the time they have together. During a time of poignant happiness, Joy reminds him that her death is inevitable. Lewis recoils from this reminder and claims that it mars the happiness of the moment. But she persists, explaining that "the pain that is coming is part of this present happiness."

When Lewis acknowledged her inevitable death and allowed her pain to permeate his love for her, he was finally able to truly enter into her life. And, in so doing, he discovered a depth and richness in love that had previously been hidden from him.

When Joy has died and Lewis's former intellectual concepts about God and the good of suffering have been shattered, he acknowledges that suffering is not good. But, he has learned, the *whole* of human life *is* good—with all of its suffering and pain. He comforts Joy's young son with his new realization: "Our future happiness is part of this present pain."

🏹 LIVING SO THAT DEATH IS NOT A DEFEAT

My father suffered a good many losses in life without knowing defeat. A loss robs us of something that we already possess. Some losses, such as the death of a loved one, leave us devastated, but not defeated. A defeat takes away from us what we hoped to gain. Failure to gain a victory or a prize is a defeat. We can suffer losses without defeat.

I live with the certainty of my own death. My death, I suppose, will be a loss for those who love me, and I can even speak of it as a loss of my own life. But it can never be a defeat. I am not in a "life-and-death" struggle, in which death can rob me of some hoped-for victory or prize.

This is what I learned from my father. He was not in competition with death as though life were a prize to be wrested out of the jaws of death. Life already had been given to him. Adversity and misfortune, joy and prosperity came and went; they were all part of the gift of his life.

One of his favorite expressions when calamity struck was, "Well, we will just have to tighten our belt and go on." I have never understood precisely what this expression meant. It may have referred to the effects of a lack of food, in which case we need to take in our belts to keep our pants from falling off a shrinking waistline.

When my father said it, I felt secure and safe. There was no panic and confusion when disasters came, even though he never had an insurance policy. As he approached what he knew was certain death from an incurable illness, he only "tightened his belt," so to speak, and lived within the narrowing limits of what he considered a fair share of life.

What is a fair share of life? The only share that I have is what I have been given. Life cannot be measured by its length, as though I have earned some right to a long life. Nor can it be measured by the amount of goods and money I can amass, as though such things somehow broadened or deepened my "share of life."

Death, I learned from my father, is part of everyone's share of life. And if death is part of my share of life, then I will not suffer defeat as though some alien power has overcome me and robbed me of meaning and value.

LIVING SO THAT DEATH IS NOT THE END

There is only one death that was not a fair share of life. That is the death of Jesus Christ, the Son of God. The living God has no share in death. The death of God would be the ultimate defeat and plunge all of life into chaos and darkness.

chapter eleven

The story of Christianity, however, begins with the birth of God in the form of a human—Jesus, the son of Mary. The Gospel of John describes Jesus as the divine Word of God "which became flesh and dwelt among us" (John 1:14). In becoming a human through the conception and birth of Jesus, God also assumed the human share of life: death.

The moment that Jesus was born, there was the certainty of his death. Although he did not know the time and manner of his death, every day of his life Jesus carried with him the knowledge that he would die. However brief or long it was, Jesus' fair share of life included death. And he had freely chosen such a fate out of love for humans.

As Jesus died in agony on the cross, his mother Mary heard his last anguished cry. The mother who had felt the first heartbeat of God in her womb now experienced the last heartbeat of her son.

Was this death a defeat? Did God lose the ultimate victory to death? No! Three days after his death, Jesus was raised to life again. The human heartbeat of God continues!

In his letter to the early Christian church, the apostle Paul—who had personally experienced the resurrected and living Jesus—almost shouts out the implications for each of us:

"Death has been swallowed up in victory. Where, O death is your victory? Where, O death is your sting?" The sting of death is sin, and the power of sin is the law. But thanks be to God, who gives us the victory through our Lord Jesus Christ.

(1 Cor. 15:54-57)

Christians believe that death is not the end of life! Instead, it is the passageway to the new and eternal life with God. Because Jesus, through his resurrection, defeated death, those who believe in him have the same power to step through death into new life.

My father knew this. He had learned well his catechism of teachings about the Christian faith. I learned to believe the same truth and to confess the same faith through my study of the catechism at church.

What the church could not teach me, however, I learned from my father. I learned what it is to die with dignity, courage, and grace. I learned not to be surprised by death, since it belongs to one's fair share of life. I learned that death is not a defeat, nor is it the end of everything.

Around many older churches, especially in villages and rural areas, are the grave markers of former parishioners. In such places, one cannot escape the reminder that worshiping God as the source of life means also coming face-to-face with the reality of death.

The cemetery adjoining my boyhood farm was separated from us by only a wire fence through which I easily could crawl back and forth. Having crossed over many times in my youthful play, I shall not be surprised to find myself crossing once more—for the last time—drawn by the view from the other side.

Just room for me to squeeze between
The lowered ceiling and divide
Just power enough to make the ridge
And, panting, gain the other side;

Just light enough to see my field
And in the shadows kiss the grass;
Just strength, just heart, just time enough,
For me, the tardy one, to pass.

chapter eleven

O hill, O strip of clearing sky,
Hold up the bars till I get by!
O lovely day—forgive my sin,
One breath of light will let me in!

(Anne Morrow Lindbergh, "Closing In,"
The Unicorn and Other Poems,
New York: Pantheon, 1956, p. 35)

The cows still stand up at midnight on Christmas Eve

n Christmas Eve, we milked the cows *before* rather than *after* supper. This may not seem a momentous event, but it was the only time during the year that my father permitted this indulgence. I say indulgence, because rising from the supper table in a warm kitchen to go out again into the cold night just to milk cows seemed unnecessary and inhuman to my boy's mind.

"Why not finish all the chores before supper so that we could stay in the house after supper?" I implored more than once. Patiently, my father would respond: "That is so that we can do our milking while your mother is washing up after supper. That way we all finish at the same time." While that answer had a good deal of virtue, it failed to satisfy my suspicion that we did it that way because his father had always done it that way! It never occurred to me to suggest that we might give mother a hand with the dishes and that way finish up at the same time as well! That argument wouldn't have changed his mind. Milking cows was a man's chore and washing up after a meal was a woman's.

On Christmas Eve, however, my father was willing to bend the rule about milking in order to accommodate a family tradition. On the night before Christmas, we always had an oyster stew supper and then went to church for the annual Christmas program. Herein lies the story.

When the last of the stew had been eaten and the last oyster swallowed with relish by my father (with something of a flourish to impress those of us who had not yet acquired the taste), he told us a story.

"My father used to tell us," my own father would say, "that if you were to go to the barn at midnight on Christmas Eve, you would see an amazing sight. At the very stroke of midnight, in honor of the birth of the baby Jesus, all of the cows will rise to their feet. They have an instinct that humans do not have. This instinct they have inherited from those animals who were in the stable where Jesus was born. It is a wonder to behold!"

Each year as the story was told, my imagination took flight. I pictured the cows that I knew so well, each one by name, standing to their feet. I wanted to see this miracle for myself! Each year I promised myself that just before midnight I would go out to the barn to see this sight. Each year, unfortunately, I would fall asleep and not wake up until morning.

Then came a year that sealed the story to my heart in a way that will never be forgotten. I was in my early teens, old enough to stay awake and go to the barn at midnight. As the hour approached, I looked out the window at the barn and thought, "I am finally going to see this miracle for myself."

But I did not go. I clearly remember deciding not to investigate this phenomenon, for I realized that I was going out of doubt and not out of faith.

Let me explain. My father's story had the power to transform ordinary things into an extraordinary image in my mind. These were ordinary cows, not religious ones. I was caught by the vision of these animals, so well known to me, suddenly rising to their feet to honor the birth of Jesus—a blind yet compelling act of devotion. This vision stirred my own childlike faith that Jesus was the gift of God and worthy of adoration and worship.

My father's story connected my ordinary and familiar world to the wondrous event of God's birth in a stable at Bethlehem. The story stimulated my imagination and lifted the rooftop off my familiar stable so that my ordinary cows could hear the extraordinary singing of angels!

As a teenager, so I thought, I had grown out of this naive faith and wished to test the validity of my beliefs. In particular, I wanted to see once and for all whether or not the cows would stand up.

It never occurred to me as a child to question *whether* the cows would stand at midnight; I only wanted to be there when it happened. Likewise, it never occurred to me to ask my father whether he had ever gone to the barn to see this event. Such is the power of a story to compel faith beyond question.

I doubt whether my father ever went to the barn at midnight on Christmas Eve. He never claimed to be describing what he had seen, rather what he had been told and what he believed because of the one who told it.

There is a certain "murderous" intention in the need to prove or disprove a story that demands faith to tell and believe. There is a kind of ruthlessness that wants to expose a belief as a myth, to be examined like the corpse of an animal one has tracked down and, finding it unfit to eat, tossed away as worthless.

As I looked out the window at the silent barn with the sleeping cows, there arose in my heart a whisper of caution. "Once you go," I told myself, "it will never be the same." Some reason beyond reason itself compelled me to pause. If the story were indeed proved to be true, I could then tell only what I had seen, not what I believe. Faith, the Bible tells us, is "the assurance of things hoped for, the conviction of things not seen."

I never did go. I have kept the faith.

For me, the cows still stand at midnight on Christmas Eve in honor of Jesus' birth. I still have a story to tell to my children and grandchildren.

What angel it was that whispered caution in my heart on that midnight so many years ago I may never know. But I will be eternally grateful. My father and I have this in common: we kept the mystery in our hearts and our faith in the story.

✈ THERE ARE TRUTHS THAT CANNOT EASILY BE TOLD

"Tell the truth," we are often urged, and thus taught to equate truth with the telling of it. There are truths that must be told; I freely acknowledge that. But there are also deeper truths that are almost impossible to express in words: like the love of a man and a woman, the bond between friends, the whisper of an angel.

The Gospel writer Luke describes how an angel announced to Mary that she would conceive a child by the power of the Holy Spirit (Luke 1:35). How does one go about explaining such a truth in words? Luke also tells us that Mary, after the wondrous events of Jesus' birth on that first Christmas, "treasured all these things and pondered them in her heart" (Luke 2:19). What else can one do with the truth of God's birth in human form but keep it as a mystery of the heart?

✈ THERE ARE TRUTHS THAT ONLY STORIES CAN TELL

A friend who was once our youngest daughter's Sunday school teacher recalls the time she told the story of how God sent ten plagues to convince Pharaoh to let the people of Israel leave Egypt. After our friend had vividly and dramatically related the story, our daughter looked her straight in the eye and demanded, "Is that *really* true?"

To this day, my friend cannot recall exactly what she said in response. Just as well. One hopes that the question was not answered in the spirit in which it was asked.

Stories contain truth, but a different kind of truth than that contained in facts. The truth by which Christians live is carried by stories. The truth by which God's Old Testament people lived was contained in stories that they passed on from generation to generation. These are stories about real flesh-and-blood people, but they are more than that: they are about God and God's actions in human history. These are stories that awaken and sustain faith. The Bible is full of such stories: it *is* such a story—one that contains the truth necessary for life.

My father was not known as a storyteller. In fact, the story about the cows standing at midnight on Christmas Eve is the only one I recall him telling. This story became for me the truth of the biblical story about the birth of Jesus. As I took my part in the Christmas pageant in that small church later on Christmas Eve, the reenactment of the story of Jesus' birth became even more real and true to me. My father's story had already awakened my faith in the truth that I now helped share.

The British philosopher of science Michael Polanyi once wrote, "Our believing is conditioned at its source by our belonging." The church could tell the story and witness to its truth. But the bond that my father had created with me instilled a capacity for faith to believe—first the truth of his simple story (because *he* told it) and then the truth of the Christmas pageant at church.

Do the cows really stand up at midnight on Christmas Eve? That is not a question that leads to faith. But it recalls a story that, through my father, the Spirit of God used to impart the truth about Jesus' birth in the heart of a young boy. And that young boy has carried that truth in his heart to this very day.

THERE ARE TRUTHS THAT CAN BE RECEIVED ONLY BY FAITH

"We walk by faith and not by sight," wrote the apostle Paul in his New Testament letter to the Corinthian Christians. Paul ought to know. He literally had been blinded by his first experience of faith.

Before he came to faith in Jesus Christ, Paul had heard the stories told by early Christians: stories about how Jesus had been killed and then rose to life, stories about how Jesus had ascended to heaven, stories about how God's Spirit had filled Jesus' closest followers on Pentecost—stories about how Jesus was the Son of God. Paul failed to see any truth in those stories: in fact, they enraged him. So furious was he that he set out to expose the stories as lies and to murder those who told them.

Suddenly, Paul had a vision of the risen Christ as he traveled to the city of Damascus. The vision caused him temporarily to lose his sight, and it changed his life. Once his sight had been returned, Paul became the most fervent Christian of them all. His vision of Jesus had given him faith in Jesus.

I doubt that Paul ever made a pilgrimage to see Jesus' empty tomb for himself or visited the place where Jesus was said to have been born. Yet he told the stories about what happened in each place a thousand times. If he ever had been tempted to "see for himself"—just to make sure—I would bet that he paused and whispered to himself (as I did at the window on that Christmas Eve): "Careful, Paul. Once you go, it will never be the same."

"We walk by faith and not by sight." The Christians' walk through life is often filled with dangers and over difficult terrain. The walk will eventually lead through "the valley of the shadow of death" (words from Psalm 23, my father's favorite psalm), but those who walk by faith need fear no evil, because God has promised to walk with them all the way.

Through the stories in this book, I have walked with you through a valley filled with sunlight and shadows, taking you along paths from my father's and my own life journey.

Unspoken Wisdom

"We read," someone once said, "so that we know that we are not alone." I hope that you have recognized some of the paths in these stories, paths that you yourself have traveled.

All that I have told you in this book is true. My father was an ordinary man, no better or worse than a hundred other men whom I knew during my boyhood. What made him special was the fact that he was my father and he taught me everything I really needed to know about life.